Pope Francis

MORNING HOMILIES

POPE FRANCIS

MORNING HOMILIES

In the Chapel of St. Martha's Guest House
March 22 – July 26, 2013

Translated by Dinah Livingstone

ORBIS BOOKS
Maryknoll, New York 10545

Founded in 1970, Orbis Books endeavors to publish works that enlighten the mind, nourish the spirit, and challenge the conscience. The publishing arm of the Maryknoll Fathers and Brothers, Orbis seeks to explore the global dimensions of the Christian faith and mission, to invite dialogue with diverse cultures and religious traditions, and to serve the cause of reconciliation and peace. The books published reflect the views of their authors and do not represent the official position of the Maryknoll Society. To learn more about Maryknoll and Orbis Books, please visit our website at www.maryknollsociety.org.

Library of Congress Cataloging-in-Publication Data

Francis, Pope, 1936-
[Sermons. Selections. English]
Pope Francis morning homilies : in the Chapel of St. Martha's guest house, 22 March-6 July 2013 / translated by Dinah Livingstone.
   pages cm
   ISBN 978-1-62698-111-9
1. Catholic Church—Sermons. I. Title.
   BX1378.7.A5 2015
   252'.02—dc23
                2014033307

Second Printing, May 2015

Contents

Introduction by Inos Biffi   *ix*

IN THE CHAPEL OF ST. MARTHA'S GUEST HOUSE   *1*

Pontifical Mass with
Vatican Gardeners and Waste Collectors   *3*
Christ Died for All   *3*
God's Patience   *4*
How Beautiful to Be Forgiven   *5*
Never Speak Ill of Others   *6*
The Grace of Tears   *8*
From Grumbling to Hope   *9*
Peace Has No Price   *10*
In the Name of Jesus   *12*
Faith Isn't for Sale   *14*
The Golden Rule of Humility   *16*
In Praise of Gentleness   *17*
Salvation according to Francis   *20*
Obedience Is Listening That Sets Us Free   *21*
God Doesn't Have a Magic Wand   *24*
No Gossip, No Fear   *26*
Slander Kills   *29*
The Spirit Can't Be Tamed   *31*

The Church Isn't a Babysitter   *33*

God Is Person   *36*

A Church Free of Ideology   *39*

Don't Give Way to the Temptation of Scandal   *41*

Christ Is the Door to the Kingdom   *43*

In the Middle of a Love Story   *46*

Magnanimity in Humility   *48*

Faith Is Not a Fraud   *51*

For a Community Open to the Values of the Spirit   *53*

Blessed Shame   *56*

Far from Worldliness   *59*

No to Slave Labor   *61*

For a Church That Says Yes   *64*

Challenging Jesus   *66*

Persecution by the Prince of This World   *69*

A Traveling Companion   *72*

Joy in Forbearance   *74*

Jesus Doesn't Exclude Anybody   *76*

Melancholy Isn't Christian   *78*

Two Ways Out for the Christian   *80*

The Holy Spirit, the Unknown   *82*

Satan Always Swindles Us   *84*

When Shepherds Become Wolves   *86*

The Pains of St. Paul   *89*

Peter's Shame   *92*

Good Manners and Bad Habits   *95*

Prayer Works Miracles   *98*

True Power Is Service   *100*

No One Should Kill in God's Name   *103*

The Salt That Gives Flavor   *105*

The Wisdom of Christians *107*

Christian Welcome *108*

God's Time *111*

The Christian's Reward *113*

The Triumphalism of Christians *116*

Eternity Won't Be Boring *118*

The Scandal of the Incarnation *121*

The Great Forgetters *123*

Let's Learn the Language of Children *126*

Life at the Bottom *128*

Unmasking Hidden Idols *130*

The Difficult Science of Love *133*

Between Amazement and Memory *135*

Doors Open to Consolation *137*

Signs of Free Giving *140*

Adolescent Progressivism *143*

The Tongue Can Kill Too *145*

True Christian Humility *148*

Christian Haste *151*

The Christian All or Nothing *153*

Loving Our Enemies *156*

The Grace of Joy and Kindness *158*

Praying the Our Father *161*

In Search of the Real Treasure *163*

The Pillars of Christian Salvation *166*

The Example of John the Baptist *168*

The Call of Abraham *171*

The Joy of Fatherhood *174*

Christians in Deed and in Truth *176*

The Mystery of God's Patience *179*

We Must Pray to the Lord with Courage   *182*
Brave in Weakness   *184*
Touching His Wounds to Profess Jesus   *187*
The Freedom of the Children of God   *190*
Mercy, Feast, and Memory   *192*
Renewal without Fear   *195*

APOSTOLIC JOURNEY TO RIO DE JANEIRO
ON THE OCCASION OF
THE XXVIII WORLD YOUTH DAY   *199*

Like Clay Pots   *201*
The Treasure and the Clay   *202*
The Wisdom of Grandparents   *204*

Introduction

✣

THE HOMILIES OF
POPE FRANCIS

With the collection and publication of the accounts of Pope Francis' *Morning Homilies*, which have appeared day by day in *L'Osservatore Romano*, it is now possible, even for those who were not present, to read a good number of them together and get to know and enjoy them as a whole.

AN ORIGINAL STYLE

Friendly talks

"Homilies" is exactly what they are, and as we know, the "homily" is a particular Christian literary form, with illustrious models in the Fathers. We think, among others, of Basil, John Chrysostom, Ambrose, and Augustine. Jean Leclercq defines it as a "friendly talk by a pastor of souls with his people during a liturgical service on a biblical text suggested by the liturgy."[1]

Of course the pithy content of these "friendly talks" by Pope

---

1 J. Leclercq, *La Liturgie et les paradoxes chrétiens* (Paris: Cerf, 1963) 208.

Francis is important. But what stands out and strikes us immediately is the originality of their style, their lively, simple language, rich with metaphors, graphic images, that involve the listeners, speak to them and engage with their actual daily lives, whose ups and downs the pope illustrates in the light of the gospel. So a language that doesn't dwell on the theological or speculative depths of the truths of faith, which of course are their source, but on their practical application. We could call it applied teaching of the Christian mystery in its everyday relevance.

An incisive language. Images and metaphors

I have touched upon the language of these homilies, in which the ideas are incisively clothed in images and metaphors. Thus it is said of the Emmaus disciples that "they were simmering their lives in the sauce of their grumbling" (April 3); of Christians who must keep facing reality, "ready, like the goalkeeper of a football team, to save the ball wherever it comes from" (April 13). The pope speaks of the true God of faith and of a "diffuse god, a god-spray, that's a bit everywhere, but we don't know what it is' (April 18); of "intellectuals without insight" and "moralists without kindness" (April 19); of "going to confession like going to the dry cleaners" (April 29); and, referring to the clergy, of "good mannered simony" that is secretly paying someone purely in order to become something (May 21); of the "pastoral border control sacrament" (May 25), which instead of opening, closes the door upon people; of the "science of tenderness" (June 7); of "making a fruit salad," by putting together "a bit of Holy Spirit and a bit of the spirit of the world" (June 10); of "adolescent progressivism" (June 12); of a "holy picture face" (June 14) which conceals our own sinfulness; of revenge that "is such a good meal when it is eaten cold" (June 18). Reminding us that we will have to leave our earthly goods here when we die, he observes, "I have never seen a moving van behind a funeral procession" (June 21).

A *"Directory of spiritual life"*

But from this language, vividly expressing his thought and immediately drawing our attention, we find in Pope Francis' homilies a wise "discernment of spirits"—to use an Ignatian term—that is, the rare acute inner penetration and psychological acumen, of someone with a habitual long familiarity with human situations, a lucid knowledge of the problems, reactions and feelings of communities and people in general. And through it shines a long experience and involvement, sometimes expressly and suggestively recalled.

That is why we don't hesitate to define it as a precious *Directory of Spiritual Life.* Thanks also to the way fundamental themes, which are both traditional and given a new freshness, are resumed and recur, the homilies offer both faithful and clergy, including bishops, a whole compendium of considered advice and vigorous ascetic directions.

A Look at the Contents

As for the contents of the individual homilies, obviously they consist of all sorts of things, as befits the literary genre of the homily. It could be said they cover the whole area of Christian life, illuminated by the principal mysteries of faith.

The beauty of being forgiven. God's kindness

1.   Just to give an indication. It seems to me that one important recurring theme is that of forgiveness, propounded in a new

and original way, which has raised intense and widespread interest. "How lovely," he said, "to be saints but also how lovely to be forgiven." The sinner in darkness must not lose hope: he "finds Jesus again, his forgiveness, the 'kindness of the Lord.' The pope invites us to "open our hearts and taste the 'sweetness' of this forgiveness," "expressed in Jesus' look at Peter when he had denied him" (March 26).

Speaking of the confessional he says: "The confessional isn't a 'dry cleaner' that removes the stains of sin, nor is it a 'torture session' where you are beaten up. Confession is in fact a meeting with Jesus and feeling his tenderness with your hand." "Confession is a meeting with Jesus who expects us as we are." We feel ashamed but "being ashamed is a virtue of the humble." We go to the Lord "with trust, joy and without deceiving ourselves" (April 29). "The problem isn't being sinners but rather not repenting of our sins." And again he returns to the look Jesus gave Peter, "such a beautiful look, so beautiful!" which makes Peter burst into tears: "a story of meetings" during which Jesus shapes the apostle's soul by love (May 17).

2. Pope Francis repeats: "The Lord loves us tenderly. The Lord is familiar with the beautiful science of tenderness. God's tenderness: he doesn't love us merely in words. He comes to us and stands close by us, and gives us his love with all possible tenderness." "Closeness and tenderness are the two ways in which the Lord loves us. He comes close and gives all his tender love even in the smallest things," which also reveals "the strength of God's love." But the pope adds: "It may sound like a heresy but it is the greatest truth: more difficult than loving God is letting ourselves be loved by him." But "that's the way to give back all that love to him": "Let him be tender and caress us." "Lord," the pope exclaims in prayer "teach me the difficult science, the difficult habit of

letting myself be loved by you, of feeling you close and feeling your tenderness" (June 7). Then he says: "The key to all prayer: to feel loved by a father, a Father, who is very close, who folds us in his arms" (June 20), who "created us, gave you life, you and me," who "has called you personally by name" (25 June), who "has set us on our way"(June 22); not a "cosmic God," but one who "in the mystery of [his] patience" "walks in step with us" (June 28).

Jesus the Savior

1.   Speaking of Jesus, Pope Francis stresses that he "alone can save" and no one else. Certainly not by consulting "fortune tellers and tarot readers" (April 5). He makes clear: "Jesus Christ didn't save us by an idea or intellectual program. He saved us with his flesh, with his own actual flesh. He lowered himself, he became human, he became flesh to the very end." Thus he offered the true image of Christian humility, which leads us to recognize our condition as sinners: "We need to recognize that we actually are sinners," "clay pots," and not present ourselves with "a holy picture face" (June 14).

2.   The pope has a special liking for the image of the "door" applied to Jesus: "There is only one door by which to enter the kingdom of God. And that door is Jesus." "The true door, the only door," "a beautiful door, a door of love," which never deceives us, and stays open for us to reach the Father. Thieves and robbers "rob glory from Jesus" and this also happens "in our Christian communities. There are these burglars, who seek their own glory, aren't there? They try to enter, while seeking their own glory" (April 22). This can happen among those who are followers of Jesus and they may even be priests

and bishops, because "that's the way to pursue a career," forgetting that it isn't possible to "take away the cross from the way of Jesus" (May 28) and that "the comfort culture" prevents us from walking "close to Jesus."

3.   The pope returns insistently to careerism "which has done great harm to the church" (May 15), and to worldly triumphalism or "triumphalist fantasies" (April 12), which are "Christianity without the cross," "a halfway Christianity" (May 29).

   And he leads us to reflect on the "the spirit of the world" that leads us to idolatry (June 6), on bitterness, on the envy loved by the devil which "corrodes the Christian community" (May 18); on "gossiping communities" that "bad-mouth others and do them down" (April 27), and on "gossiping Christians": "What a lot of gossip there is in the church!" says Pope Francis. "What a lot we Christians gossip!" "That's tearing each other to pieces, wounding one another"; "Gossip is destructive in the church, yes, destructive. It has something of the spirit of Cain: killing your brother by your tongue." And this is done "with good manners. But in this way we become Christians with good manners and bad habits! Christians who are polite but nasty" (May 18).

4.   Other themes are: hypocrisy, which is the "tongue of the corrupt," who "do not love the truth. They only love themselves and so they try to deceive people, to involve others in their lies, their falsehoods. They have lying hearts; they can't tell the truth": it is the same language "as that used by Satan in the wilderness when he tempted Jesus" (June 4). The pope doesn't hesitate to speak of "hypocrisy in the church": "What a lot of harm it does to all of us!" because "all of us are capable of becoming hypocrites" (June 19).

Then there is his invitation not to "retreat into grumbling," which "hurts our hearts" (April 3); not to be afraid to "build bridges," to be ready to "listen to everybody," since "Jesus doesn't exclude anyone" (May 8); to be patient, since patience "restores our youth, it make us younger" (May 7); to allow ourselves to be swept along by the "urgent haste of the Christian message," which is "apostolic zeal," aroused by "something so wonderful," which is "God's love who delivered his Son to death for me." It is "not striding ahead to make converts and statistics" but "the message of reconciliation," that Christ became sin for me and the sins are there in his body, in his mind." "This is crazy but it is beautiful: it's the truth," Pope Francis exclaims in an outburst of admiration. Hence the thought that "Christian peace is a restless peace, not a tranquil peace" (June 15).

5. Jesus is the door to the Father, says the pope. And as well as himself he has also given us his wounds as a door. "Jesus' wounds are still present upon Earth," "priestly wounds of intercession." And on them the pope deftly bases the theology of prayer and the christological meaning of charity. Prayer is "a going out of ourselves," which occurs "with the intercession of Jesus himself, who stands before the Father and shows him his wounds." "His wounds are his prayer of intercession." So we must "go out of ourselves twice": "toward the wounds of Jesus"; and "toward the wounds of our brothers and sisters. And this is the way Jesus wants us to follow in our prayers" (May 11).

The Church in the Father's heart

1. Speaking of the church, Francis recalls the different aspects of its mystery. He begins first of all with: "The church be-

gins in the Father's heart," the start of a "love story" that
isn't yet finished. It is carried on by the Holy Spirit, who
"troubles us" because he moves us, makes us get going
(April 16). The church "doesn't grow by its human strength"
and so we should not boast of its "quantity." Otherwise it
"becomes a bit bureaucratic," it "loses its main substance
and risks becoming an NGO [Non-governmental organi-
zation]. The church is not an NGO. It's a love story" (April
24). The pope repeats: "when we find apostles who want
to create a rich church, a church without the free gift of
praise, that church grows old, it turns into an NGO, it has
no life." In fact, "the church isn't a cultural organization,
or even a religious or social organization. It isn't like that."
It is the confession "that Jesus is the Son of God, come in
the flesh. That's the scandal and that's why they persecuted
Jesus." The cause of martyrdom is when we don't want to
be "reasonable Christians, social Christians, just doing good
works," but followers of the cross (June 1).

That doesn't cause sadness. On the contrary: thanks to
the Holy Spirit, "author" and "creator of joy," Christians
overcome their mistrust and receive the gift of true freedom: freedom and joy, which make us "go out of ourselves
to praise God, to spend our time praising" (May 31).

2.   The church, which "has her memory, the Lord's passion"
(May 13)—which means that we must also be mindful—is
entrusted to Jesus Christ. "We can guard the church, we
can take care of the church, can't we?" asks the pope. And
he answers: "We must do that by our work. But more important is what the Lord does: he is the only one who can
look the Evil One in the face and conquer him. 'The prince
of this world is coming against me and he can do nothing.' If we don't want the prince of this world to get hold

of the church, we must entrust it to the only one who can defeat the prince of this world" (April 30). For that prince "doesn't want us to be saved," he "hates us and stirs up persecution," and "you can't parley with the prince of this world" (May 4). Certainly, it isn't without significance that today the pope should return to the subject of the devil, who has almost disappeared from theology and preaching.

3.   And still on the subject of the church: she "is a mother" and we are "a family in the church who is our mother"; a mother not "a babysitter, who looks after the child to make it go to sleep" (April 17). So the church must be wary of ideology. Ideologists "falsify the gospel." The "doctors only respond with their heads" and discuss God's word as "academics," thus losing through their lack of humility "the way to love and also the way to beauty" (April 19).

We have focused on the church; but there is one strand, a golden thread, that runs through all these homilies and it is the Madonna: the mother "who covers the people of God with her cloak" (April 15), who "brings our greatest joy, brings Jesus" (May 31), who "always brings us to Jesus" (April 5), and to whom prayer is habitually addressed.

We have tried to offer a flavor of these "family talks" by Pope Francis as a foretaste. Now it remains to read them and enjoy them as a whole.

—*Inos Biffi*

Pope Francis

MORNING HOMILIES

IN THE CHAPEL OF ST. MARTHA'S GUEST HOUSE

PONTIFICAL MASS WITH
VATICAN GARDENERS AND WASTE COLLECTORS

Friday, March 22, 2013
JER 20:10–13; JN 10:31–42

When we have a heart of stone, we pick up real stones and stone Jesus Christ in the persons of our brothers and sisters, especially those who are weakest. So we must open our hearts to love, Pope Francis said, commenting on the readings of the day during the Mass celebrated on March 22 in the chapel of St. Martha's Guest House.

It was a simple celebration to which the pope invited the staff of the gardening and waste collection services of the Vatican City State, improvising a short homily based on the passage from John's gospel which tells the story of the Jews who wanted to stone Jesus.

CHRIST DIED FOR ALL

Saturday, March 23, 2013
EZ 37:21–28; JN 11:45–57

On this morning too, Saturday, March 23, Pope Francis invited some of the Vatican City workforce to the morning

3

Mass in the chapel of St. Martha's Guest House. There was another group of the Vatican City State gardening and waste collection staff who had not been able to take part with their work colleagues in the Mass celebrated by the pope on the first Friday morning reported in yesterday's edition. With them there were some greenhouse workers and about fifteen sisters of the Devout Disciples of the Divine Master, who work in the Vatican City telephone exchange.

In his homily the Holy Father offered a brief reflection on the liturgical readings of the day and, in particular, on the passage from John's gospel (11:45-56), where we read the words of Caiaphas the high priest to the chief priests and Pharisees assembled in the Sanhedrin, together with the evangelist's comment: Jesus was about to die for the nation, and not for the nation only but to gather into one the dispersed children of God. Jesus died for his people and he died for everyone. But, said the pope, this should not be taken in a collective sense: it means that Jesus died for each one of us individually. So every Christian must say: Christ died for me.

This is Jesus' greatest expression of love for each of us. And when we become aware of this love, the pope stressed, we should feel thankful. With such a passionate and deep thank you as to cause tears of joy on the faces of each of the faithful.

GOD'S PATIENCE

Monday, March 25, 2013
IS 42:1–7; JN 12:1–11

G od's patience was the core of Pope Francis' homily during the Mass he concelebrated in the early hours of the morning, today March 25, in the chapel of St. Martha's Guest House.

Commenting briefly on the liturgical readings, the pope said that in the description of the suffering servant in the book of the prophet Isaiah, we have "the image of Jesus," of his meekness and his patience. This patience of God is a mystery, and we see it in the behavior of Jesus himself, unlike that of Judas, he added, referring to the story of the anointing at Bethany according to John's gospel (12:1-11). God is patient like the father of the prodigal son, who waited every day for his return. And if we apply this to ourselves, the pope concluded, just two words will leap from our hearts: thank you.

As in the previous recent Masses, many people took part who work in Vatican offices. Among them were those who work in the photograph service of the newspaper.

How Beautiful to Be Forgiven

Tuesday, March 26, 2013
Is 49:1–6; Jn 13:21–33, 36–38

Pope Francis celebrated Mass in the chapel of St. Martha's Guest House on the morning of Tuesday, March 26. On that day he wanted the other priests staying in this Vatican residence to be with him at the altar. The day before they had returned to their rooms, after leaving them for a few weeks for the cardinals who had come to Rome for the conclave. There were about forty of them, among whom were officials of the Secretariat of State and other bodies and dicasteries. A priestly family which the pope said he felt he belonged to. To them, before giving the final blessing, he expressed his thanks.

Commenting briefly on the gospel passage from John (13:21-33; 36-38), in which Jesus speaks of Judas' betrayal and reminds Peter that he will deny him three times, the pope shared with those present his thoughts on two words: "night" and the "sweetness" of Christ's forgiveness. It was night when Judas left the supper room. And the Holy Father stressed that it was night both outside and inside him. But, the pope recalled, there is another night, a "temporary night," with which we are all familiar and in which, beyond the darkness, there is always hope. It's the night of the sinner who finds Jesus again, his forgiveness, "the Lord's tenderness." Pope Francis invited us to open our hearts and taste the "sweetness" of that forgiveness. The same sweetness that was expressed in Jesus' look at Peter when he had denied him. "How beautiful to be saints," he concluded, "but also how beautiful to be forgiven."

Among the faithful present there were some sisters of the Secular Institute of Schönstatt resident in Rome. At the end of the celebration, after a few minutes of silent prayer spent sitting at the back of the chapel, Pope Francis greeted each person individually. And he gave the priests resident at St. Martha's a big chocolate egg bearing the papal coat of arms.

Never Speak Ill of Others

Wednesday, March 27, 2013
Is 50:4–9; Mt 26:14–25

Speaking ill of someone means selling them. As did Judas when he sold Jesus for thirty pieces of silver. In his brief homily at the Mass celebrated on the morning of Wednesday, March 27, in the chapel of St. Martha's Guest House, Pope Francis took his inspiration from the gospel passage from Matthew, which foretells

Judas' betrayal. The pope warned against malicious gossip. Succinctly and explicitly he said: "Never speak ill of other people." Present at the celebration, as by now is customary, were some Vatican staff.

The pope gave them a reflection on the action of Judas, one of Jesus' friends, who didn't hesitate to sell him to the chief priest. "Jesus becomes like merchandise: he is sold." He was sold at that moment, he stressed, and also so many times in the market of history, the market of life, in the market of our lives. When we choose the thirty pieces of silver, we let Jesus go.

When we visit an acquaintance and the talk turns to backstabbing and malicious gossip, according to the pope, "this is selling," and the person we are talking about "becomes merchandise." "I don't know why," he said, "but there is a murky enjoyment in gossip." We start by saying nice things "but then comes the gossip. And we begin tearing the other person to pieces." And we should realize that every time we behave like this "we are doing the same thing Judas did." When he went to the chief priests to sell Jesus, his heart was closed, he had no understanding, no love, and no friendship.

And so Pope Francis returned to one of his favorite subjects, forgiveness. "We think about and ask for forgiveness," because what we do to the other person, our friend, "we do to Jesus. Because Jesus is in this friend." And if we realize that our talk can harm someone, "let us pray to the Lord, let us speak with the Lord about this, for the good of the other: Lord, help him." It isn't for me, he concluded, "to carry out justice with my tongue. Let us ask this grace of the Lord."

At the end of the celebration the Holy Father became absorbed in prayer at the back of the chapel. But he was waiting at the exit for all who were present to greet them one by one: as always, he had a word for everyone, an encouragement, a smile and good wishes for Easter.

THE GRACE OF TEARS

Tuesday, April 2, 2013
ACTS 2:36–41; JN 20:11-18

Pope Francis invites us to ask for a special grace: the grace of tears. Because "tears are what prepare us to see Jesus." He explained this on the morning of Tuesday, April 2, during the Mass celebrated in the chapel of St. Martha's Guest House, at which, as is now the custom, a group of Vatican staff was present, including the Vatican City State Police and the Fire Fighters.

The pope commented on the episode in John's gospel where Mary Magdalene says "I have seen the Lord!" Before that she had washed his feet with her tears and dried them with her hair (cf. John 20:11-18). The pope recalled that Jesus forgave this woman's many sins because "she loved much." He returned to the witness given by this woman— "despised by those who thought of themselves as righteous"—at the moment when she had to face "the collapse of all her hopes." Her love was no more and she wept. It was the moment of darkness. But she didn't say "I've failed." She simply wept. Sometimes in our lives the glasses through which to see Jesus are tears. There is a moment in our lives when only tears prepare us to see Jesus. And what is this woman's message? "I have seen the Lord."

This is an example for the course of our lives. In our lives, the pope said, "all of us have been through moments of joy, pain, sadness; we have all suffered these things. But, I ask, did we weep? In our darkest moments did we weep? Did we have that gift of tears that prepare our eyes to see the Lord? Seeing this woman weeping we too can ask the Lord for the grace of tears. It's a beautiful grace. A beautiful grace. We can weep for everything: for the good, for our sins, for gratitude, we can also weep for joy; weep for joy! That joy which we have asked to have in heaven and of which we now have a foretaste. Weeping. Weeping prepares us to see Jesus. And the Lord gives us, all of us, the grace to be able to say in our lives, 'I have seen the Lord.' 'Why? Did he appear to you?' 'I don't know; but I've seen him, I've seen him in my heart. I've seen him alive that way.' That is the witness. 'I've seen the Lord.' Beautiful! And all of us can bear this witness: 'I live like this because I have seen the Lord.'" At the end of the Mass the pope spent time greeting all who were present.

FROM GRUMBLING TO HOPE

Wednesday, April 3, 2013
ACTS 3:1–10; LK 24:13–35

Grumbling hurts the heart. Complaints are ugly; and not only complaints against others "but also those against ourselves, when everything feels bitter to us." With these thoughts about everyday life Pope Francis updated the story of the disciples on the road to Emmaus—told by Luke the evangelist (24:13-35)—in his homily on Wednesday, April 3, during the usual Mass in the chapel of St. Martha's Guest House. Staff of the Domus Romana Sacerdotalis [Roman Priest House] were present at the Mass.

In his commentary on the gospel the pope dwelt on the disciples' dismay at their teacher's death, which was so great, the pope said, that they thought it better to leave the city. "But the poor things kept talking about it, didn't they? And they were grumbling. We could call that day the grumbling day." But all their discussions did was lock them up inside themselves. And in their hearts they were thinking: "We had so much hope, but it has all come to nothing." And in that situation, said the pope, "they were simmering their lives in the sauce of their grumbling, and carried on like that."

That's how it relates to us. "I think," he added, "that often when difficult things happen, when the cross comes to us, we too run the risk of locking ourselves up in grumbling." And yet, even at that moment the Lord "is close to us. But we don't realize it. He also speaks to us but we don't hear him." For us grumbling is "a sort of security: this is my truth, my failure. There is no more hope. And with these thoughts the disciples continued on their way." And "what did Jesus do? He was patient with them. First, he listened to them, then he slowly explained to them. Then in the end, he let himself be seen." Jesus, added the pope, "does the same with us. Even in our darkest moments he is always with us, he walks along with us. And in the end he makes us aware of his presence." Returning to complaints which "are ugly" because "they take away our hope," Pope Francis urged us not to play "the game of living by grumbling," because the Lord's presence became plain "when he broke the bread" and the disciples were able to see "the wounds." Then "he disappeared." We must always trust in God, who "always accompanies us on our road" even in our darkest hours. "We are sure, we are sure," he concluded, "that the Lord never abandons us: So let's not retreat into grumbling: it hurts our hearts."

Peace Has No Price

Thursday, April 4, 2013
Acts 3:11–26; Lk 24: 35–48

Peace can't be bought or sold: it's a gift of God. And we must ask for it. Pope Francis reminded us of this on the morning of

Thursday, April 4, when he spoke of the "amazement" shown by the Emmaus disciples at Jesus' miracles. He was commenting on the gospel passage from Luke (24:35-48), which was read in the liturgy of the usual morning Mass in the chapel of St. Martha's Guest House, in the presence of Vatican staff, on that morning about fifty managers and operatives of the Vatican Press.

"The disciples who witnessed the healing of the lame man and who now see Jesus," said the pope, "are somewhat beside themselves, not because of a mental illness but from amazement." But what is this amazement? "It means," said the Holy Father, that "yes, we are somewhat beside ourselves, for joy: that is great, very great. It isn't mere enthusiasm: fans in a football stadium are enthusiastic when their team wins, aren't they? It isn't just enthusiasm, it is something much deeper: it's the amazement we feel when we meet Jesus."

That amazement, the pope explained, "is the beginning of the Christian's habitual state." Of course, he added, we can't always live in a state of amazement, but that condition is the beginning, which allows "a mark to be made on the heart and brings spiritual consolation." In fact the Christian's state of mind should be spiritual consolation, despite problems, pains and illnesses. "The ultimate degree of consolation," said the pope, "is peace: we begin with amazement, then the quieter tone of this amazement, and from this consolation comes peace." Even in the most painful trials, the Christian never loses "the peace and presence of Jesus" and "with a little courage, we can say to the Lord: 'Lord, give me the grace that is the mark of a meeting with you: spiritual consolation.'" And above all, he stressed, "never lose peace." We look at the Lord who "suffered so much on the cross, but didn't lose peace. That peace is not ours: it can't be bought or sold." It's a gift of God that we must ask for. Peace is like "the ultimate degree of that spiritual consolation, which begins with joyful amazement." So we must not let ourselves "be deceived by our fantasies or any other delusions, which lead us to think that these fantasies are the reality." In fact, it's more Christian "to believe that reality can't be so beautiful." The pope concluded by asking for the grace of spiritual consolation and peace, which "begins with this joyful amazement at meeting Jesus Christ."

IN THE NAME OF JESUS

Friday, April 5, 2013
ACTS 4:1–12; JN 21:1–14

The name of Jesus alone is our salvation. Only he can save us. And no one else. Let alone modern "fortune tellers" with their improbable tarot prophecies which fascinate and delude modern people. It was upon the name of Jesus that Pope Francis based his reflection on the morning of April 5, the Friday after Easter, during the Mass celebrated in the chapel of St. Martha's Guest House, in the presence of the sediari pontifici [the Papal Chair-bearers] and managers, staff and religious of the Fatebenefratelli [Brothers Hospitallers of St. John of God], who work in the Vatican Pharmacy.

The pope took his cue from the first reading, from the Acts of the Apostles (4:1-12), to reflect on the value and meaning of the name of Jesus. The passage tells the story of Peter and John, who had been arrested because "they were announcing in Jesus the resurrection of the dead." They were taken before the Sanhedrin. When they were asked about how they had healed the lame man near the Temple gate, Peter replied: "We did it in the name of Jesus Christ." In the name of Jesus, repeated the pope, adding: "He is the Savior; this name, Jesus. When you say Jesus, he is the one," the one who works miracles. "And this name is with us in our hearts."

In John's gospel too, the pope added, the apostles were upset "because they had caught no fish all night. When the Lord asked them for something to eat," they replied no, quite roughly. But "when the Lord said to them, 'Throw the net on the right hand side of the boat and you will find some,' perhaps they thought of that time when the Lord had told Peter to go fishing and he had answered: 'We haven't caught anything all night, but in your name I will go!'"

Then returning to the Acts of the Apostles, Pope Francis explained that "Peter tells the truth when he says 'we did it in the name of Jesus,'" because his reply was inspired by the Holy Spirit. In fact, he continued, "we can't confess Jesus, we can't speak of Jesus, and we can't say anything about Jesus without the Holy Spirit." It's the Holy Spirit "who impels us to confess Jesus or speak of Jesus or have confidence in Jesus." And it's he who is beside us "on our life's road, always."

Then the pope spoke about a personal experience, his memory of a man, the father of eight children, who had worked for thirty years in the archbishop's office in Buenos Aires. "Before he went out, before he went to do anything that he had to do," said the pope, "he always whispered to himself 'Jesus!' Once I asked him, 'Why do you always say Jesus?' 'When I say Jesus,' this humble man replied, 'I feel strong; I feel I can work, because I know he is beside me, that he is looking out for me.'" Yet, the pope stressed, this man "had not studied theology, he had only the grace of baptism and the strength of the Spirit." And his witness, Pope Francis said to those present, "did me so much good. The name of Jesus. There is no other name. Perhaps it will do good to all of us" who live "in a world that offers us so many 'saviors.'"

Sometimes, "when there are problems," he remarked, "people don't trust in Jesus but in other realities." Maybe they resort to so-called fortune tellers "because they resolve situations" or perhaps "they go to consult tarot readers" to find out and understand what to do. But salvation can't be found in fortune tellers or tarot readers: it lies "in the name of Jesus. And we must bear witness to this! He is the only Savior."

Then the pope referred to the role of the Virgin Mary. "The Madonna," he said, "always brings us to Jesus. Invoke the Madonna, and she will do what she did at Cana: 'Do what he tells you!'" She "always brings us to Jesus. She was the first to act in the name of Jesus." Finally, the pope concluded by expressing a wish: "I'd like us on this day, which is a day in Easter week, of the resurrection of the Lord, to think this: I entrust myself to the name of Jesus; I pray, 'Jesus, Jesus!'"

Faith Isn't for Sale

Saturday, April 6, 2013
Acts 4:13–21; Mk 16:9–15

"To find martyrs it isn't necessary to go to the catacombs or the Coliseum. Martyrs are living now, in so many countries. Christians are persecuted for their faith. In some countries they can't wear a cross: if they do, they are punished for it. Today in the twenty-first century, our church is a church of martyrs." Pope Francis gave his homily on the courage of witnessing to the faith, which is non-negotiable and not for sale to the highest bidder, during the Mass celebrated on the morning of Saturday, April 6, in the chapel of St. Martha's Guest House.

Pope Francis began his homily with a joke. Commenting on the passage from Mark's gospel (16:9-15), which tells of Jesus' appearances to Mary Magdalene, the Emmaus disciples, and the eleven apostles, he said: "When I read this gospel, I think perhaps St. Mark didn't like Mary Magdalene much, because he recalls that the Lord had cast seven devils out of her, doesn't he? It was a question of liking . . . " Nevertheless he gives a reflection on her faith: "a grace" and "a gift from the Lord" that can't be kept silent—and so it extends "to all peoples" as the collect of the Mass says—"because we are not attached to a fantasy" but "to a reality which we have heard and seen." The pope referred to a passage in the Acts of the Apostles (4:13-21) from the first reading of the Mass. Ordered by the high priests and Pharisees not to speak of Jesus, Peter and John, he said, "remained firm in their faith," saying: "We can't be silent about what we have seen and heard."

Their testimony, he added, "makes me think of our faith, and how is our faith? Is it strong? Or is it sometimes a bit like rosewater, a faint faith? When difficulties come, are we brave like Peter or a bit lukewarm?" Peter, said the pope, teaches us that, "faith can't be negotiated. It has always been so in the history of the people of God, there is this temptation to water down our faith," maybe "just a bit." But our faith, he explained, "is as we say it in the Creed." So we have to overcome "the temptation to be 'just like everyone else,' not to be so rigid" because "that's the start of a way that ends in apostasy." In fact, "when we start to dilute our faith, to negotiate the faith, to sell it to the highest bidder, we start on the road to apostasy, of unfaithfulness to the Lord."

But "the example of Peter and John helps us, gives us strength." As does the example of the martyrs in the church's history. They are the ones "who say, 'We can't be silent,' like Peter and John. And this gives strength to us whose faith is sometimes a bit weak. It gives us the strength to go on in life with this faith that we have received, this faith which is the gift the Lord gives to all peoples."

The pope concluded by suggesting a daily prayer: "Lord, thank you so much for the faith. Guard my faith, make it grow. May my faith be strong and brave. And help me at the time when, like Peter and John, I have to declare it in public. Give me courage."

THE GOLDEN RULE OF HUMILITY
Annunciation of the Lord

Monday, April 8, 2013
Is 7:10–14; Lk 1:26–38

Humility is the "golden rule": For the Christian "getting on" means "lowering yourself." And it's the road of humility, chosen by God himself, along which love and kindness walk. The pope recalled this in his homily during the Mass he celebrated on the morning of Monday, April 8, in the chapel of St. Martha's Guest House.

The whole history of faith, said the pope, is of humility and "speaks to us of humility." And so it was for the historical event of Jesus' birth. It seems as if God wanted every event "to happen secretly, not to be made public," as if it were "covered by the shadow of the Holy Spirit." That's why, he added, "everything happens on the way of humility. God humbly lowers himself: he comes to us and lowers himself. And he continues to do so right to the cross."

At the moment of the annunciation, said the pope, Mary lowers herself: she doesn't understand very well but she is free: she understands only the essential. And she says yes. She is humble: "God's will be done." And "Joseph her betrothed—they weren't married yet—also lowers himself and brings this great responsibility upon himself." Joseph, continued the pope, "also says yes to the angel who told him what had happened in a dream."

Mary and Joseph's style shows that "all God's love takes the way of humility to come to us. A humble God who wants to walk with his people." The pope referred to the book of Deuteronomy, saying: "I have carried you in the desert as a father carries his child. God, so humble and kind. A patient God. This is different from the attitude of idols; they are strong, they make themselves felt: I give the orders here!"

"Our God is true, because he isn't a pretend God, he is true;

he isn't a wooden god made by human beings, he is true and he prefers to proceed like that, along the road of humility." The Holy Father went on to explain: "All this love comes by way of humility. Being humble doesn't mean walking along the road with lowered eyes like this, no, no. It's God's own humility that teaches us, the humility of Mary and Joseph." And, he added, "it's the humility of Jesus which ends on the cross. And that's the golden rule for a Christian: to carry on, to advance and to lower ourselves. We can't go by any other road. If I don't lower myself, if you don't lower yourself, you are not a Christian. 'But why should I lower myself?' To let all God's kindness come along this road, which is the only one he has chosen—he hasn't chosen any other—which will end on the cross. And then in the triumph of the resurrection."

"The Christian's triumph," he concluded, "goes by this way of self-abasement. I think that's the word: lowering ourselves. Let's look at Jesus who begins by lowering himself in such a beautiful mystery. Let's look at Mary and Joseph. And let us ask for the grace of humility. But when Paul says: think that others are better than you; sometimes it's difficult to feel like this. But Paul has in mind a mystery, this road, because in the depths of his heart he knows that love only walks along this way of humility." In fact, "if there is no humility, love is blocked, it can't carry on. So let us ask for the grace of humility from the Madonna, St. Joseph, and Jesus."

In Praise of Gentleness

Tuesday, April 9, 2013
Acts 4:32–37; Jn 3:7–15

The temptation to gossip about others and batter them with words is always just around the corner. Even in the family, among friends and in the parish, "where the catechesis ladies fight with the Caritas ladies." These are "everyday temptations"—"the enemies of gentleness" and of unity among people and in the Christian community—"which happen to everyone, including me." Pope Francis put us on our guard against this attitude during the Mass celebrated on the morning of Tuesday, April 9, in the chapel of St. Martha's Guest House.

The pope pointed to the way of gospel gentleness to allow the Spirit to work and regenerate us to a "new life" of unity and love. "Let us ask for the grace," he said, "not to judge anyone" and to learn "not to gossip behind other people's backs"—it would be "a great step forward"—seeking to be "kind to one another," "respectful," and gently "making way for others."

"In the prayer at the beginning of Mass," said the pope in his homily, "we asked the Lord, through the power of the risen Jesus, to show the world the fullness of the new life. The new life begins with the resurrection of Jesus. And this is what Jesus said to Nicodemus. You must be 'born from above,' have a new beginning." Nicodemus, the pope explained, referring to the gospel passage in John (3:7-15), "is a learned man. A bit earlier in the gospel he had answered Jesus: but how can a man be born again? Can he return to his mother's womb and be born again? But Jesus was speaking in another dimension: being 'born from above,' born of the Spirit. It's a new birth, it's that new life, that power, that beauty of new life which we asked for in our prayer. It's the new life we have received in baptism, but which must develop."

"We must do our utmost," the pope reiterated, "to let this life develop into the new life. And what will this new life be like? It's not that we say today, 'Yes I was born today, that's it, and I'll begin again.' It's a journey, a difficult journey. It needs hard work. But it's also a journey that doesn't depend on us alone. Mainly it depends on the Spirit, and we must open up to the Spirit so that he can create this new life in us."

"In the First Reading in today's liturgy," said Pope Francis, commenting on the passage from the Acts of the Apostles (4:31-34), "we get a foretaste, a preview of what 'new life' will be, what 'new life' ought to be. All those who had become believers were of one heart and one mind. Single-minded, single-hearted: unity, that unity, that unanimity, that harmony of feelings in love, mutual love. Thinking 'the others are better than me,' and that's fine, isn't it?"

"But reality," the pope explained, "tells us that this doesn't happen automatically after baptism. It's work to be done as we go through life, work to be done by the Spirit in us and our own faithfulness to that Spirit." And "that gentleness in the community is a somewhat forgotten virtue. Being gentle, making way for others. There are so many enemies of gentleness, aren't there? Gossip to start with. When we prefer to gossip, gossip about other people, do them down. These are everyday things that happen to all of us, to me as well."

"They are temptations of the Evil One," he continued, "who doesn't want the Spirit to come to us and make this peace, this gentleness in Christian communities. We visit the parish and the catechesis ladies are fighting with the Caritas ladies." And "there is always this infighting. It happens in the family and in our local area. But also between friends. And that isn't the new life. When the Spirit comes and we are born to a new life, he makes us gentle and kind. Not to judge anyone: the only judge is the Lord." So the advice is to "keep quiet. And if I have to say something, I will say it to him or her, but not to the whole neighborhood, only to the one who can mend the situation."

"That," Pope Francis concluded, "is just one step in the new life, but it's a step to be taken daily. If, by the grace of the Spirit we manage never to gossip, that will be a big step forward. And it will do all of us good. Let us ask the Lord to show us and the world the beauty and fullness of this new life, this being born of the Spirit, who comes into the community of the faithful and enables us to be gentle, kind to one another. To be respectful. Let us ask this grace for all of us."

SALVATION ACCORDING TO FRANCIS

Wednesday, April 10, 2013
ACTS 5:17–26; JN 3:16–21

"The Lord doesn't save us by a document, by a decree, but he has saved us," and continues to save us "by his love," restoring "dignity and hope" to human beings. At the usual morning Mass, celebrated in the chapel of St. Martha's Guest House on Wednesday, April 10, Pope Francis spoke about Christian salvation and its deepest meaning: God's love for us who through his only-begotten Son "became one of us, went about among us."

Commenting on the collect, the pope stressed that in fact the first prayer of the Mass said to the Lord: "You did two things at Easter; you restored humanity to its lost dignity." And consequently "you have given us hope." That, he explained, "is salvation. The dignity of being God's children restores our dignity and also gives us hope. It's a dignity that progresses, until the final meeting with him. This is the way of salvation, and it's beautiful; only love can do it. We are worthy, we are women and men of hope."

Sometimes it happens that "we want to save ourselves and think we can do so. 'I save myself!' We don't put it like that but in our lives that's what we do." For example, when we think "I can save myself by money. I am secure, I've got money, there's no problem… I have dignity: the dignity of a rich person." But, said Pope Francis, all that "isn't enough. Let us remember the gospel parable of that man who has a full barn and says: 'I'll get another one, so that I can have more and then sleep soundly.' And the Lord answers: 'Fool! Tonight you will die.' That kind of salvation won't do. It's provisional, merely apparent salvation." It's like when we delude ourselves that we can "save ourselves with vanity, with pride," believing we are "powerful," "masking our poverty, our sins with our vanity and pride." All those things come to an end, but true salvation has to do with the dignity and hope we have received through God's love, he added, referring to the passage from John's gospel (3:16-21) which had been read earlier, saying that he has sent his Son to save us.

Hence the pope invited us to make "an act of faith," saying: "Lord, I believe. I believe in your love. I believe your love has saved me. I believe your love has given me that dignity I didn't have. I believe your love gives me hope." Then it becomes "beautiful to believe in love" because "that's the truth. It's the truth of our lives."

An invitation to believe in God's love, repeated by the pope at the end of his homily, with a closing appeal to "open our hearts for this love to come into them, fill us and press us to love others."

Obedience Is Listening That Sets Us Free

Thursday, April 11, 2013
Acts 5:27–33; Jn 3:31–36

God is non-negotiable. And faith has no room for the "lukewarm," who are "neither good nor bad," who seek a modus vivendi with the world by the compromise of a "double life." This is what Pope Francis said in his homily at the Mass celebrated on the morning of Thursday, April 11, in the chapel of St. Martha's

Guest House, at which the management and editorial staff of the Osservatore Romano were present. As well as journalists on the daily paper, there were also staff from the periodical editions and the general management.

Pope Francis explained in his homily that in the readings for the Mass "the word 'obey' occurs three times: they talk about obedience. The first time is when Peter replies: 'We must obey God rather than men,'" to the Sanhedrin, as is related in the Acts of the Apostles (5:27-33).

So what does it mean, asked the pope, "obedience to God? Does it mean that we must be bound like slaves? No, because anyone who obeys God is free and not a slave! And how is that? I obey, I don't do what I want so am I free? It sounds like a contradiction. But it isn't a contradiction. In fact, the word 'obey' comes from the Latin and means listening to, heeding the other person. Obeying God is listening to God, having an open heart to carry on along the way God points. Obedience to God is listening to God. And that sets us free."

Commenting on the passage from the Acts of the Apostles, the pope recalled that Peter facing those scribes, priests and even the high priest and the Pharisees, was called upon to "make a decision." Peter "heard what the priests and Pharisees were saying, and he heard what Jesus was saying in his heart. 'What shall I do?' He says: 'I will do what Jesus tells me, not what you want me to do.' And he went ahead with that."

"In our lives," said Pope Francis, "we also hear proposals that do not come from Jesus, that do not come from God. And of course, our weaknesses sometimes take us along that road. Or along another which is even more dangerous: we come to terms, a bit of God and a bit of me. We make an agreement and so we move forward in life with a double life: partly the life we feel Jesus is telling us to lead and partly the life we hear the world telling us about, the powers of the world and so much else." But this is a "no-go" system. In fact "in the book of Revelation, the Lord says: this won't do, because like this you are neither good nor bad, you are lukewarm. I condemn you."

The pope warned against this temptation: "If Peter had said to those priests, 'Let's talk it over as friends and come to a modus vivendi' perhaps things would have been all right." But it wouldn't have been a choice taken out of "the love that comes when we listen to Jesus." A choice that has consequences. "What happens," continued the pope, "when we listen to Jesus? Sometimes those against us get angry and it ends in persecution. At this moment, as I said, we have so many sisters and so many brothers who are being persecuted for obeying, listening, hearing what Jesus is asking them. Let us always remember those brothers and those sisters who have put themselves in the fire and tell us with their lives: 'I want to obey, to walk along the way that Jesus tells me.'"

In today's liturgy "the church invites" us to "walk along Jesus' way" and "not to listen to the proposals made to us by the world, proposals to sin, or those so-so, half and half proposals" that, he reiterated, "won't do" and "won't make us happy."

In this choice of obedience to God and not to the world, without giving way to compromise, the Christian isn't alone. "Where," asked the pope, "can we find help to walk along the way of listening to Jesus? In the Holy Spirit. We are witnesses of this fact: it's the Holy Spirit whom God has given to those who obey him."

So, he said, "It's the Holy Spirit within us who gives us the strength to carry on." John's gospel (3:31-36), read to us in the Mass, assures us in a beautiful phrase: "'He whom God has sent speaks the words of God, for he gives the Spirit without measure.' Our Father gives us the Spirit, without measure, to listen to Jesus, to hear Jesus and to walk the way of Jesus."

Pope Francis ended his homily with an invitation to be brave in life's different situations. "Let us ask for the grace of courage. We will always have sins: we are all sinners." But we need "the courage to say: 'Lord, I am a sinner, sometimes I obey worldly things, but I want to obey you, I want to walk your way.' Let us ask for this grace, always to walk the way of Jesus and when we don't, to ask for forgiveness: the Lord forgives us because he is so good."

GOD DOESN'T HAVE A MAGIC WAND

Friday, April 12, 2013
ACTS 5:34–42; JN 6:1–15

"Triumphalist fantasies" are "a great temptation in Christian life." But God "doesn't act like a fairy with a magic wand" to save us in an instant. Rather, he uses the way of perseverance, because "he saves us in time and in history," "on our journey day by day." That was the thought offered by the pope during the Mass celebrated on Friday morning, April 12, in the chapel of St. Martha's Guest House.

Referring to the passage in the Acts of the Apostles (5:34-42) read in the first reading, the pope mentioned Gamaliel, "a wise man" because "he gives us an example of how God acts in our lives. When all those priests, Pharisees, and doctors of the law were so nervous, furious about what the apostles were doing, and wanting to kill them, he said: But stop a moment! And he recalls the stories of Judas the Galilean and Theudas, who didn't succeed in doing anything: they said they were the Christ, the Messiah, saviors but then they failed. 'Give time time,' says Gamaliel."

"It's good advice," Pope Francis explained, "for our lives as well. Because time is God's messenger: God saves us in time, not in an instant. Sometimes we think the Lord comes into our lives, and changes us. Yes, we can change: this is called conversion. 'I want to follow you, Lord.' But it must be a journey. So the Lord saves us in history, our personal history. The Lord isn't like a fairy with a magic wand. No. He gives you the grace and says, as he said to all those he healed: 'Get up and walk.' He says it to us too: 'Go forward in your life, bear witness to all that the Lord does with us.'"

So we must shun "a great temptation in Christian life: triumphalism. It's a temptation, said the pope, suffered also by the apostles. For example, when Peter says to the Lord, but, Lord, I will never deny you, never! The Lord says to him: be quiet, before the cock crows you will deny me three times." That's precisely the temptation to "triumphalism: to believe that everything has been done in an instant. No, it begins in an instant: it's a great grace, but we have to carry on along life's way."

Even after the multiplication of the loaves—as told in John's gospel (6:1-15)—there is the temptation to triumphalism. "When the people saw the sign that he had done, they began to say: 'This is indeed the prophet who has come into the world. When Jesus realized that they were about to come and take him by force to make him king,' he withdrew." So here we have "triumphalism: Ah, this is the king! And then Jesus rebukes them: you follow me, not in order to listen to my words, but because I gave you food to eat."

"Triumphalism," the pope explained, "isn't from the Lord. The Lord came on Earth humbly. For thirty years he led his life, grew up like a normal child, endured the test of work, and also the test of the cross. And then at the end he rose again. The Lord teaches us that not everything in life is magic, that triumphalism isn't Christian."

"What the wise Gamaliel said is true: Leave them alone, time will tell!" And "we too," the pope continued, "say to ourselves: 'I want to go straight to the Lord, by his way.' But this isn't something that happens in an instant; it takes a lifetime, every day. When I get up in the morning: 'Lord, to walk with you, to walk with you.' This is the grace we must ask for: the grace of perseverance."

So, he concluded, it's a matter of "persevering along the way of the Lord until the end, every day. I don't mean start all over again every day: no, carry on along the road. Always carry on. A difficult way that takes effort but also with so much joy. It's the way of the Lord."

"Let us ask," he urged, "for the grace of perseverance. And that the Lord may save us from triumphalist fantasies. Triumphalism isn't Christian, not from the Lord. The everyday way in God's presence, that is the way of the Lord. Let us go that way."

No Gossip, No Fear

Saturday, April 13, 2013
Acts 6:1–7; Jn 6:16–21

To solve life's problems you have to look reality in the face; like the goalkeeper on a football team, you have to save the ball wherever it comes from. And you mustn't give way to fear or the temptation to grumble, because Jesus always stands beside each one of us, even and especially at the most difficult moments. This is what Pope Francis said in the Mass celebrated on the morning of Saturday, April 13, in the chapel of St. Martha's Guest House. Among those present were members of the police and fire service, and some disabled people who were attending a Vatican congress.

In the passage from the Acts of the Apostles (6:1-7) read in the first reading, the pope explained, "here is a piece of the history of the church's early days: the church was growing, the number of disciples was increasing," but "at that moment problems began." In fact, "the Greek speakers complained against the Hebrew speakers" because their widows were being neglected in the daily distribution. "Life," he continued, "isn't always calm and sweet" and "the first thing they do is grumble, gossip about one another: 'But look, there is this . . . ' But that doesn't lead to any solution, it doesn't bring a solution. Instead, the apostles with the help of the Holy Spirit, reacted well. They called together the group of disciples and spoke. That's the first step: when there are difficulties, we need to look at them well, take them on board and speak about them. Never just hide them. Life is like that. Life has to be taken as it comes, not how we would like it to come." Pope Francis, resorting to an apt metaphor that he enjoys said, "It's a bit like the goalkeeper on a football team, isn't it? He has to save the ball wherever it comes from. That's the reality." So the apostles "spoke among themselves and came up with a good proposal, a revolutionary proposal, because they said: 'But we are the apostles, the ones whom Jesus chose.' But that's not enough. They realized that their priority should be prayer and the service of the word. 'And we must do something else about the daily distribution to the widows.' So they decided to appoint the deacons."

"Rather a risky decision at that moment," the pope added. "But the Holy Spirit had pushed them to do that. So they did it. They chose the deacons, they made a decision. They didn't say: 'We'll think about it tomorrow. Patience!' No, no. They took the decision and the result was fine: 'The word of God continued to spread; the number of disciples increased greatly in Jerusalem.' That's fine. When there are problems, we need to take them on board and the Lord will help us to solve them."

So "we shouldn't be afraid of problems. Jesus himself says to his disciples: It's me. Don't be afraid, it's me! Always. In all life's difficulties, problems, new things we have to deal with: the Lord is here. We may make mistakes, of course, but he is always near us and says to us: you've made a mistake, get back on the right path."

A problem, said the pope, can't be resolved if we just say, "I don't like this" and begin to "grumble and gossip." And "it isn't the right attitude simply to disguise life or put makeup on it. No, no. Life is as it is. That's reality. And that's how God wants it to be or allows it to be. But it's as it is, and we have to take it as it is. The Spirit of the Lord will give us the solution to problems."

"In the gospel too," the pope explained, commenting on the passage just read from St. John (6:16-21), "something similar happens. The disciples were all pleased because they had seen that those five loaves went on forever. They had given so many people food to eat. They set sail toward the other shore, in their boat, and a strong wind blew up. The sea became rough and they were afraid. They were in difficulties. And the Lord came to them to help them. They were frightened and he said to them: 'Don't be afraid, it's me.' That's always what Jesus says: in difficulties, at dark moments, moments when everything is black and dark and we don't know what to do, even when the darkness is in our soul. Life is like that. Today may be like that, in that darkness. But the Lord is there. Let's not be afraid! Let's not be afraid of difficulties, let's not be afraid when our hearts are sad and dark. Let's take things as they come, with the spirit of the Lord and the help of the Holy Spirit. And so we go forward, safely along the right way."

Pope Francis concluded his homily with an invitation to ask "the Lord for this grace: not to be afraid, not to disguise life," so that we are able "to take life as it comes and try to solve the problems as the apostles did. And to try to meet Jesus who is always beside us, even in life's darkest moments."

SLANDER KILLS
Monday, April 15, 2013
ACTS 6:8–15; JN 6:22–29

Slander destroys God's work, because it's born of hatred. It's the daughter of the "father of lies" and tries to destroy people, and alienate them from God. In the *Barber of Seville* Basil sings that slander is a little breeze, but for Pope Francis it's a mighty wind. He said so on the Monday morning of April 15, during the usual Mass celebrated in the chapel of St. Martha's Guest House. Among those present were staff and managers of the Telephone and Internet Services of the Vatican City State.

Slander is as old as the world and is referred to in the Old Testament. Think of the story of Queen Jezebel and Naboth's vineyard, or of Susanna with the two judges. When it proved impossible to get something "in the right way, the holy way," people resorted to slander, which is destructive. And this, said the pope, "makes us think: we are all sinners, all of us. We all have sins. But slander is something else." It's a sin but it's also something more because "it tries to destroy God's work and is born of something very evil: it's born of hatred. And the hate-maker is Satan." Lying and slander go hand in hand because they need one another to proceed. And doubtless, added the pope, "where there is slander, there is Satan himself."

Then Pope Francis took his inspiration from Psalm 118 [119] in the liturgy of the day to explain the state of mind of the good person who is slandered. "Even though princes sit plotting against me, your servant will meditate on your statutes. Your decrees are my delight." The just man in this case is Stephen, the first martyr, who came into the first reading from the Acts of the Apostles. Stephen "looks to the Lord and obeys the law." He is the first in a long series of witnesses to Christ who have studded the history of the church. Not only in the past, but also in our time there are plenty of martyrs. "Here in Rome," added the Holy Father, "we have so many testimonies of martyrs, beginning with Peter. But the time for martyrs hasn't come to an end: today we can even say that actually the church has more martyrs than in the early centuries."

In fact the church "has many women and men who are slandered, persecuted and threatened out of hatred for Jesus, hatred of the faith." Some are killed because "they teach the catechism," others because "they carry the cross." Slander finds its way into so many countries where Christians are persecuted. There are brothers and sisters of ours, he insisted, "who suffer today in this time of martyrs. We must remember that. They are persecuted out of hatred: it's the devil himself who sows hatred in those who carry out the persecutions."

Speaking again about St. Stephen, the pope recalled that he was one of the deacons ordained by the apostles. "He proves full of grace and power," added the pope, "and he performed great miracles, great signs among the people, and furthered the gospel. Then some people began to debate with him about Jesus: whether Jesus was the Messiah or no." That discussion became heated and "those who debated with him couldn't withstand the wisdom and the spirit with which he spoke." So what did they do? Instead of asking him to explain they resorted to slander in order to destroy him. "As they were not winning the clean fight, the fight between good people, they resorted to fighting dirty, to slander." They found false witnesses who said: "This man never stops saying things against this holy place and against the law of Moses, against this, against that." Just as they had done with Jesus.

In our time characterized by "so many spiritual upheavals" the pope invited us to reflect on a medieval icon of the Virgin. The Madonna who "covers the people of God with her cloak." The first Latin antiphon of the Virgin Mary is also *sub tuum pre-*

sidium. "We pray to the Madonna to protect us," said the pope, "and in times of spiritual upheaval the safest place is under the Madonna's cloak. Indeed, she is the mother who looks after the church. And in this time of martyrs she is the protector, she is the mother."

So the pope invited us to put our trust in Mary, to turn to her with the prayer that begins "under your protection" and remember that ancient icon where "she covers her people with her cloak: she is the mother."

THE SPIRIT CAN'T BE TAMED

In Prayer for the Victims of the Boston Bombing

Tuesday, April 16, 2013
ACTS 7:51—8:1; JN 6:30–35

"Today is Benedict XVI's birthday. We are offering the Mass for him so that the Lord may be with him, strengthen him and give him great comfort." At the beginning of the eucharistic celebration he held on Tuesday, April 16, in the chapel of St. Martha's Guest House, the pope's first thought was for his predecessor on his eighty-sixth birthday. During the Mass the victims of the Boston bombing were also remembered. The pope used his homily to warn those who give way to the temptation to resist the Holy Spirit. "The Spirit," he stressed with gentle firmness, "can't be tamed."

The Holy Father referred to the Second Vatican Council, which, he said, "was a fine work of the Holy Spirit. Think of Pope John: He seemed like a good parish priest and he was obedient to the Holy Spirit," carrying out what the Spirit wanted. And the pope wondered whether "after fifty years we have done all that the Spirit asked us to do at the Council" to continue that "growth of the church that the Council was."

"No," was his reply. "We are celebrating this anniversary," he explained, almost raising "a monument" to the Council, but we are mainly concerned that "it should not give us trouble. We don't want to change." In fact there's "more": there are voices which want to go backwards. That's called "being obstinate," that's called trying "to tame the Holy Spirit," that's called becoming "foolish and slow of heart."

The pope took his cue from the first reading, taken from the Acts of the Apostles (7:51-58). He began by saying: "Stephen's words are strong: 'You stiff-necked and uncircumcised in heart and ears. You always resist the Holy Spirit. As your fathers did, so do you. Which of the prophets did your fathers not persecute? They killed those who foretold the coming of the Righteous One, and now you have become his betrayers and murderers. You have killed the prophets,' then you built them a fine tomb, a monument, didn't you? I don't know if it's put just like that. And then you venerated them, but only after you had killed them. Here we see that resistance to the Holy Spirit. Jesus said the same but a bit more gently to the Emmaus disciples: 'How foolish and slow of heart you are to believe all that the prophets have declared!'"

Among us too, added the pope, we find that resistance to the Holy Spirit. In fact, "to put it plainly, the Spirit troubles us. Because," he explained, "he moves us, he makes us get going, he presses the church to go forward. And we are like Peter at the transfiguration: 'Ah, how good it's to be here like this, all together!' As long as it doesn't give us any trouble. We want the Holy Spirit to soothe us. We want to tame the Holy Spirit. And that won't do. Because he is God, he is that wind that comes and goes, and you don't know where. He is the power of God; he is the one who gives us the encouragement and strength to go forward. But really go forward! And that's a nuisance! We prefer to be comfortable. You could say, 'But, Father, that happened in those days. Now we are all happy with the Holy Spirit.' No, that's not true! There is still that temptation today." As we see from the experience of the reception of Vatican II.

"In our personal lives, in our private lives as well," the pope continued, "the same thing happens: the Spirit urges us to follow a path more in accordance with the gospel, and we say : 'No Lord, it's all right as it is...' Hence the decisive commandment: "Do not resist the Holy Spirit." Because "it's the Spirit who sets us free, with the freedom of Jesus, with the freedom of the children of God! Do not resist the Holy Spirit: that's the grace I would like us all to ask from the Lord; obedience to the Spirit, that Spirit who comes to us and makes us go forward along the path of holiness, the beautiful holiness of the church. The grace of obedience to the Holy Spirit."

THE CHURCH ISN'T A BABYSITTER

Wednesday, April 17, 2013
ACTS 8:1–8; JN 6:35–40

The church should not be like "a babysitter who looks after the child to make it go to sleep." If it were, it would be "a drowsy church." Anyone who has come to know Jesus has the strength and the courage to proclaim him. Likewise anyone who has received baptism has the strength to walk, to go forward, to preach the gospel. And "when we do that the church becomes a mother who gives birth to children" capable of bringing Christ into the world. This, in sum, was the thought proposed by Pope Francis this morning, Wednesday, April 17, during the Mass celebrated in the chapel of St. Martha's Guest House. It was attended by many staff of the Institute for Works of Religion.

In his homily commenting on the first reading taken from the Acts of the Apostles (8:1-8), the pope recalled that "after Stephen's martyrdom, a violent persecution broke out against the church in Jerusalem. We read in the book of Acts that the church was calm, in peace, with love among them, and the widows were looked after. But then came persecution. This is what tends to happen in the life of the church: going from peace to persecution." And that happens because, he explained, that was what Jesus' own life had been like. In the wake of the persecution, continued the pope, they all fled, except the apostles. The Christians "went away. Alone. Without priests or bishops: alone. The bishops, the apostles, were in Jerusalem to show some resistance to the persecution."

Nevertheless, those who had fled "went from place to place, announcing the word." The pope wanted to focus the attention of his listeners on them. They "had left their homes, perhaps taking little with them; they had no security, but they went from place to place announcing the word. They took with them the wealth they had: their faith. The wealth the Lord had given them. They were simple faithful, barely baptized a year or perhaps a bit longer. But they had the courage to go and announce the gospel. And they were believed! They also worked miracles. 'For unclean spirits, crying with loud shrieks, came out of many who were possessed, and many others who were paralyzed or lame were cured.' And in the end: 'There was great joy in that city!' Philip was also there. These Christians, who had not been Christians very long, had the strength, the courage to proclaim Jesus. They proclaimed him in words but also by their lives.

They aroused curiosity: 'But who are these people?' And they answered: 'We have known Jesus, we have found Jesus and we are bringing him to you.' They only had the strength of baptism. And their baptism gave them that apostolic courage, the strength of the Spirit."

The pope's reflection then turned to people today: "But what about us? Do we believe in this? That baptism is enough to preach the gospel? Or do we hope that the priest, or the bishop will say... what about us?" Too often, the pope noted, the grace of baptism is kind of set aside and we shut ourselves up within our own thoughts and concerns. "Sometimes we think: 'No, we are Christians: we have received baptism, we have been confirmed, made our first communion ... and so our identity card is all in order. So now we can sleep soundly, we are Christians.' But where is that strength of the Spirit to drive you forward?" asked the pope. "Are we faithful to the Spirit to proclaim Jesus by our lives, our witness and our words? When we do this, the church becomes a mother church who gives birth to children," the church's children who bear witness to Jesus and the power of the Spirit. But, the pope warned, "when we don't do so, the church becomes not a mother but a babysitter, who looks after the child to make it go to sleep. It becomes a drowsy church. Let's think of our baptism, the responsibility of our baptism."

And to strengthen his case, Pope Francis recalled an episode that took place in Japan in the first decades of the seventeenth century, when Catholic missionaries were driven out of the country and the communities remained without priests for more than two centuries. No priests at all. When the missionaries returned they found a living community in which all were baptized, catechized, and married in church! And even those who had died had received Christian burial. But, the pope continued, "there was no priest there! Who had done all this? Those who were baptized!"

That's the great responsibility of those who are baptized: "to proclaim Christ, take the church forward, the mother church who gives birth to children. Being a Christian doesn't mean pursuing an office career in order to become a lawyer or a mediocre Christian; no. Being a Christian is a gift that makes us go forward with the strength of the Spirit to proclaim Jesus Christ."

Finally, the pope turned his thoughts to the Madonna who has always accompanied Christians with prayer when they are persecuted or scattered. "She prayed a lot. But also encouraged them: 'Go on, do things…!'"

"Let us ask the Lord," he concluded, "for the grace to become baptized Christians who are brave and certain that the Spirit in us, which we received at baptism, is always pressing us to proclaim Jesus Christ, by our lives, our witness and also our words."

GOD IS PERSON

Thursday, April 18, 2013
ACTS 8:26–40; JN 6:44–51

Speaking to God is like speaking to persons: Father, Son, and Holy Spirit. Because this is our God, who is one and three. He is not an indefinite, diffuse God like something sprayed a bit all over the place. That was the gist of Pope Francis' reflection in his homily given during the Mass celebrated this morning Thursday, April 18, in the chapel of St. Martha's Guest House. Taking part in the Mass were managers and officers of the Vatican Public Safety Inspectorate.

It is the Lord who "speaks to us of faith," the pope began his homily. He tells us "to believe in him. But first of all he tells us something else: 'No one can come to me unless the Father who sent me draws him.' Going to Jesus, finding Jesus, knowing Jesus is a gift from the Father. Faith is a gift. A gift we received at baptism but can then develop during our lives, develop in our hearts, develop in the works we do. Faith is a gift, and anyone who has this faith has eternal life. We may ask ourselves: 'Have we got faith?' 'Yes, yes: I believe in God.' 'But what God do you believe in?' 'But in God!' How often we hear that 'in God.' A diffuse god, a god-spray, that's a bit everywhere, but we don't know what. We believe in God who is Father, who is Son, who is Holy Spirit. We believe in persons, and when we speak to God we are speaking to persons: either I speak to the Father, or I speak to the Son, or I speak to the Holy Spirit. And that is the faith."

Then referring to the first reading, taken from the Acts of the Apostles (8:26-40), the pope focused on the figure of the Ethiopian eunuch, the treasurer of Queen Candace, who had a faith that was still not very mature or stable, "the beginnings of faith." But "he had good intentions. He had come to Jerusalem to pray, to worship God, and he was reading the prophet Isaiah. He was rather troubled in his mind. The Father had done that to him in order to draw him to Jesus. And when Philip comes up to him and asks him: 'Do you understand what you are reading?' he answers no. And when Philip tells him about Jesus this man feels it is good news. He feels joy. He begins to feel a special joy. And his joy was so great that when he saw water he said: 'Baptize me now! I want to follow Jesus!'"

This, Pope Francis stressed, is something that should make us reflect: "Let's think about it. He was not a man of the street, a common man. He was a treasury minister, wasn't he? We may think he was rather attached to money. We may also think that he was a careerist because he had given up fatherhood for his career. But all that collapses in the face of the Father's invitation to meet Jesus. That's faith. And then Jesus tells us what his way is like; he tells us of the attitudes those who follow him must have: in the Beatitudes and then in our behavior. 'To follow me these are the things you must do: the Beatitudes.'" To which are added "the attitudes described in Matthew 25 on the Last Judgment: 'I was hungry and you gave me food, I was thirsty and you gave me drink, I was sick and you visited me' (cf. Matthew 25:31-46). These are the attitudes belonging to Jesus' disciples. Anyone who has faith has eternal life, has life. But faith is a gift, it's the Father who gives it to us. We have to continue along this way."

It might also happen to us, the pope said, that we are going along that way while we are absorbed in our own thoughts. What's more "we are all sinners and we always have some things that are not right." Nevertheless, the Lord forgives us "if we ask him for forgiveness: and even before that without discouraging us!" So it's possible that on that road the same thing might happen to us as happened to the Ethiopian eunuch. Once they had come up again from the water after the baptism, Pope Francis said, the Holy Spirit snatched Philip away and he "didn't see him anymore. And he went on his way full of joy."

It was the joy of faith, "the joy of having met Jesus, the joy that only Jesus gives us, the joy that brings peace: not the peace given by the world but the peace Jesus gives. That's our faith," which makes us "strong, makes us joyful," and is fed throughout life by "little daily meetings with Jesus."

At the end of the Mass, after the prayer to St. Michael the archangel, patron of the State Police, the pope thanked all those present "for the service you give to society. A difficult service, a service for the common good, for the common peace. A service that is dangerous, too, and is for the sake of life. A service which, as we asked the archangel Michael, requires an upright mind, a vigorous will, honest feelings, and calmness. Thank you very much for this service. May the Lord bless you greatly."

A Church Free of Ideology

Friday, April 19, 2013
Acts 9:1–20; Jn 6:52–59

Ideology falsifies the gospel and also ensnares the church. So during this morning's Mass celebrated on Friday, April 19, the pope asked us to pray "for the Lord to free the church from any ideology."

Commenting on the day's readings, the first taken from the Acts of the Apostles (9:1-20) and the second from John's gospel (6:52-59), Pope Francis reflected on the voice of Jesus, interpreted by some "with the heart" and by others "with the head." And he warned against those who, today too, interpret Jesus' words "with the head" and not the heart: "those ideologists who try to interpret whatever the Lord says according to the dominant ideologies and end up falsifying the gospel."

"Jesus speaks," the pope began. "Jesus speaks to Paul, Jesus speaks to Ananias, and Jesus also speaks to the doctors of the law. It's the voice of Jesus that says to Paul: 'Why are you persecuting me?' It's the voice of Jesus that goes to Ananias and says: 'Get up and go to the street called Straight, and at the house of Judas look for a man of Tarsus named Paul.' It's the voice of Jesus that speaks to the people and also to the doctors of the law, and says that anyone who doesn't eat his flesh and drink his blood won't be saved."

Jesus' voice "tells us something and goes straight to the heart. It passes through our minds and goes to the heart. For Jesus seeks our conversion. And here are the answers given to the Lord's voice in today's readings. Paul: 'Who are you, Lord?' Then Ananias says: 'But Lord, I have heard from many about this man, how much evil he has done to your believers,' and he humbly gives the Lord an account of Paul's *curriculum vitae*. The others, the doctors, respond differently, discussing among themselves. They end up saying to him: 'You are mad!' and among themselves they say: 'But how can a man give his flesh to eat?'"

The pope discussed these different responses. "The first two, Paul and Ananias, answer like the great names in the history of salvation, like Jeremiah, Isaiah. Moses himself had his difficulties: 'But Lord, I don't know how to speak. How can I go to the Egyptians and say this?' And Mary too: 'But Lord, I am not married!' These are the replies given in humility by those who welcome God's word with their hearts."

On the other hand, "the doctors only respond with their heads. They don't know that the word of God speaks to the heart; they know nothing about conversion. They are 'academics.' They are the great ideologists" who don't understand that Jesus' words are spoken to the heart "because they are words of love, beautiful words which bring love and cause us to love." Anyone who doesn't understand this bars the way to love and also the way to beauty.

"Ideologists," the bishop of Rome explained, are those who in the gospel story start "disputing hotly among themselves: 'How can this man give us his flesh to eat?' All a problem for the mind! And when ideology enters the church," the pope said, "when ideology enters the mind, nothing of the gospel is understood." Thus everything is interpreted according to the sense of duty rather than the sense of that conversion to which "Jesus invites us." And those who follow the path of duty "load it all on the shoulders of the faithful as a burden."

"Ideologists falsify the gospel," declared the pope, adding: "Every ideological interpretation, wherever it comes from, from whichever side, is a falsification of the gospel. And these ideologists—we have seen it in the church's history—end up becoming intellectuals without insight and moralists without kindness. And let's not speak of beauty, because they don't understand that at all." On the other hand, "the way of love, the way of the gospel is simple: it's the way the saints have understood! The saints are the ones who take the church forward," those who follow "the way of conversion, the way of humility, love, the heart, the way of beauty."

"Let us pray to the Lord today," the pope concluded, "for the church: that the Lord may free her from any ideological interpretation and open the church's heart, the heart of our mother the church, to the simple gospel, to that pure gospel that speaks to us of love, that brings love and is so beautiful! And also makes us beautiful with the beauty of holiness. Let us pray today for the church."

Don't Give Way to the Temptation of Scandal

"Satellite" Christians Don't Make the Church Grow

Saturday, April 20, 2013
Acts 9:31–42; Jn 6:60–69

A church made up of Christians free of the temptation to complain against Jesus as "too demanding," but above all free from the "temptation to scandal," is a church that gathers strength, carries on and grows in the way pointed out by Jesus. It was for this church that Pope Francis asked us to pray, on Saturday morning, April 20, during the Mass celebrated in the chapel of St. Martha's Guest House. About twenty volunteers working in the St. Martha pediatric dispensary in the Vatican and many families attended.

The pope's exhortation was the conclusion of his homily's reflection on the liturgical readings for the day. The passage from the Acts of the Apostles (9:31-42), he began, "tells us about a time when the church was at peace. It was at peace in all Judea, Galilee, and Samaria. A moment of peace. And it also says: It gathered strength, walked on and grew." This was a church that had suffered persecution but in that period it was gathering strength, went forward and grew. Pope Francis said it's the life of the church that "should go like that: gathering strength, going forward, and growing." And for that to be possible "we have to make pacts, do deals, things like that, don't we?"

But how does the church gather strength, go forward and grow? "In the fear of the Lord and the comfort of the Holy Spirit," the pope replied replied. This is the environment in which the church moves, the air that it breathes, "walking in the fear of the Lord and with the comfort of the Holy Spirit." And that is just what "God in the beginning had asked our father Abraham: 'Walk in my presence and be irreproachable.' That's the style of the church. To walk in the fear of the Lord. It's a sense of worship, the presence of God, isn't it? The church walks like that and when we are in God's presence we don't do nasty things or take nasty decisions. We are before God. In joy and happiness. That's the comfort of the Holy Spirit, that's the gift the Lord has given us. That comfort makes us go forward."

Then the pope referred to John's gospel (6:60-69), which uses the verbs "murmur" and "be scandalized." "Many of Jesus' disciples," he said, "began to murmur and be scandalized. Murmur and be scandalized." Some of them went away saying: "'This man is a bit peculiar, he says hard things and we can't. … It's too great a risk to go that way. We are sensible people, aren't we? Let's step back and not stay so close to him.' Perhaps these people had a certain admiration for Jesus, but from a distance. Let's not get too mixed up with this man, because he says rather strange things. These people don't stand firmly in the church, they don't walk in God's presence, they don't have the comfort of the Holy Spirit. They don't make the church grow. They are only sensible Christians: they keep their distance. They are, so to speak, satellite Christians, who make a little church to suit themselves. To put it in Jesus' own words in Revelation, they are lukewarm Christian."

The lukewarmness that develops in the church is that of those who follow their own good sense, which often coincides with common sense. They are those who proceed with a prudence that the pope didn't hesitate to define as "worldly prudence," a temptation for many. "I think," added the pope, "of so many of our brothers and sisters, who at this very moment are bearing witness to the name of Jesus, even to the point of martyrdom. These are not satellite Christians: they walk with Jesus along the way of Jesus. These know perfectly well what Peter says to the Lord, when the Lord asks him: 'Do you also want to go away, to be satellite Christians?' Simon Peter answered him: 'Lord, to whom shall we go? You have the words of eternal life.' So from having been a large group they become a rather smaller group, but a group of those who know very well that they can't go anywhere else, because only he, the Lord, has the words of eternal life."

So walk with Jesus without fear along the way he points. That was Pope Francis' invitation. At the end of his homily he asked us to pray during the Mass "for the church, so that it may continue to grow, gather strength, walk in the fear of God and with the comfort of the Holy Spirit. May the Lord free us from the temptation to that 'good sense,' the temptation to murmur against Jesus, because he is too demanding, and from the temptation of scandal."

CHRIST IS THE DOOR TO THE KINGDOM

Burglars, Thieves, or Robbers Are Those Who Try To Get In Another Way

Monday, April 22, 2013
ACTS 11:1–8; JN 10:1–10

There is only one door by which to enter the Kingdom of God. And that door is Jesus. Anyone who tries to get in another way is "a thief" or "a robber." Or he is "a housebreaker who thinks only of his own advantage," his own glory and robs the glory from God. During the Mass celebrated this morning, Monday, April 22, in the chapel of St. Martha's Guest House, Pope Francis returned to Jesus as the center of human life and reiterated that our religion is not a "negotiable" religion. His audience included a group of technical staff from the Vatican Radio and staff from the Holy See Press Office.

Commenting on the readings from the liturgy of the day, taken from the Acts of the Apostles (11:1-18) and John's gospel (10:1-10), the pope pointed out that "the word 'enter' is repeated in them. First, when Peter returns to Jerusalem, he is reproached: 'You entered a house of Gentiles.' Then Peter tells the story, tells how he went into that house. And Jesus is very explicit on this point: 'Anyone who doesn't enter the sheepfold through the door, is not a shepherd.'" To enter the kingdom of God, the Christian community, the church, "the door," the pope explained, "the true door, the only door is Jesus. We must go in by that door. And Jesus is explicit: 'Anyone who doesn't enter the sheepfold through the door—which he says "I am"—but gets in another way is a thief or a robber,' someone who wants to make a profit for himself."

This, he noted, "also happens in Christian communities. There are those burglars, aren't there? Those who seek their own ends. And consciously or unconsciously they try to enter; but they are thieves and robbers. Why? Because they rob the glory from Jesus, they seek their own glory. And that's what Jesus said to the Pharisees: 'You give glory to one another...' Religion as a kind of transaction, isn't it? 'I give glory to you and you give glory to me.' But such people have not entered through the true door. The door is Jesus, and anyone who doesn't enter through it is making a mistake."

But how to understand that the true door is Jesus? "Take the

Beatitudes and do what they say," replied the pope. So "be humble, be poor, be gentle, be just." And when anyone suggests anything different, "don't listen. The door is always Jesus and anyone who enters through that door isn't mistaken." Jesus is "not only the door: he is the way, he is the road. There are so many paths, perhaps easier ones," but they are deceptive, "they are not true, they are false. Jesus alone is the way. One of you might say: 'Father, you are being fundamentalist!' No. Simply that Jesus said this: 'I am the door,' 'I am the way' to give us life. Quite simply. He is a beautiful door, a door of love, a door that doesn't deceive us, isn't false. He always tells the truth. But with tenderness, with love."

Unfortunately, noted the Holy Father, human beings continue today to still be tempted by what in the beginning was the original sin, that is "to want to have the key to interpret everything, the key and the power to make our own way, whatever it might be, to find our own door, whatever it might be. And that is the first temptation: 'You will know everything.' Sometimes we are tempted to want too much, to be masters of ourselves and not humble children and servants of the Lord. And this is the temptation to seek other doors or windows through which to enter the kingdom of God." But "it can only be entered through the door that is called Jesus," through that door which leads us to "the way that is called Jesus and leads us to the life that is called Jesus. All those who do anything else, says the Lord, who climb up to get in through a window, are 'thieves and robbers.' He is simple, the Lord. He doesn't speak in a difficult way: he is simple."

In conclusion, the pope invited those present to pray for "the grace to always knock at that door," which is sometimes closed. We are sad, desolate and "we have problems knocking, knocking at that door." The pope invited us to pray to find the strength "not to go looking for other doors which seem easier, more comfortable, more accessible," and always to go looking "for the door that is Jesus. Jesus never deceives us, Jesus doesn't trick us, Jesus isn't a thief, he isn't a robber. He gave his life for me. Each of us must say this: 'You who gave your life for me, please, open, so that I can enter.' Let us ask for this grace. Always to knock at that door and say to the Lord: 'Lord, open, because I want to enter through that door. I want to go in through that door and not by another.'"

IN THE MIDDLE OF A LOVE STORY

The Church Is Not an Organization

Wednesday, April 24, 2013
ACTS 12:24–13:5; JN 12:44–50

The church is a love story and we are part of it. But for that very reason when too much importance is given to organization, when offices and bureaucracy predominate, the church loses her true heart and risks becoming a mere NGO. The love story to which Pope Francis referred during the Mass celebrated on Wednesday morning, April 24, in the chapel of St. Martha's Guest House, is the story of the church as a mother. The church's motherhood, he said, grows and spreads in time and is not yet finished, as it is driven, not by human forces, but by the force of the Holy Spirit.

As usual the pope commented on the readings for the day, taken from the Acts of the Apostles (12:24–13:5) and from John's gospel (12:44-50). "The first reading," he noted, "begins with these words: 'The word of God continued to advance and gain adherents.' This is the church's beginning when it's growing and spreading throughout the world." This fact might be valued by some in purely numerical terms; they are pleased that there are "more proselytes," "more members" for the enterprise. They might even stoop to "doing deals to achieve growth."

On the other hand, "the way Jesus wanted for his church," said the pope, "is a different one: it's the way of difficulty, the way of the cross, the way of persecution." And that makes us think: "But what is this church? What is this our church, because it seems that it isn't a human enterprise, but something else." Once again the answer is in the gospel, in which Jesus "tells us something that may throw light on this question: 'Anyone who believes in me doesn't believe in me but believes in him who sent me.'" So Christ, he explained was "sent, dispatched by someone else!" When he points out the program for living, the way of life to the twelve apostles, he does so "not from himself" but "from him who sent me."

It's the beginning of the church, the pope continued, "which starts in the Father's heart. He was the one to have the idea. I don't know whether he had an idea: the Father had love. And he began this love story, this long-term love story which isn't yet finished. We, women and men, are in the middle of a love story. Each of us is a link in this chain of love. And if we don't understand that, we don't understand anything about the church. It's a love story."

For, the pope recalled, Jesus said so himself: "The greatest commandment is this: love." In it are contained the church, the law, and the prophets. "But," he added, "some Christians made mistakes for historical reasons, they mistook the way, they raised armies, they made wars of religion. But that's another story, which isn't this love story. We too learn through our mistakes how the love story goes."

But then, he asked, how does the church grow? "Jesus put it simply: like a grain of mustard seed, like yeast in flour, without making a sound. The church grows, we could say, from below, slowly." And when people boast "about quantity," about organization and offices, and when "it becomes rather bureaucratic, the church loses her essence and risks becoming an NGO. The church is not an NGO. It's a love story."

He explained: "All these things are necessary, offices are necessary," but "they are only necessary up to a point," that is, "as a help to this love story." But when "the organization comes first, love collapses, and the poor church becomes an NGO. And that's not the way."

"So how does the church grow?" he asked again. "It isn't by soldiers, like that head of state who asked how many armies the pope had," he replied. The church doesn't grow through its army: its strength "is the Spirit, the Holy Spirit, love. The Father sends the Son and the Son gives us the strength of the Holy Spirit in order for us to grow, go forward."

So the church is not an organization but "she is a mother." And noting the presence of so many mothers at the Mass, Pope Francis turned to them directly and asked: "What do you feel if someone says to you: 'But you are the organizer of your household'?" anticipating the reply "'No, I am the mother!' And the church is a mother too." And by the power of the Spirit, "together we are all one family in the church who is our mother. That's how to explain this first reading: 'God's word grew and spread.' That's how it grows. That explains what Jesus says: 'Anyone who believes in me doesn't believe in me but in him who sent me.' The Father who began this love story."

"Let us ask the Madonna, who is a mother," he concluded, "to give us the grace of joy, spiritual joy to carry on in this love story."

MAGNANIMITY IN HUMILITY

Feast of St. Mark, Evangelist

Thursday, April 25, 2013
1 PT 5:5–14; MK 16:15–20

Magnanimity in humility. That's the Christian lifestyle which truly wants to bear witness to the gospel to the ends of the Earth. Pope Francis outlined this way of being "missionaries in the church" this morning, Thursday, April 25, during the now usual Mass in the chapel of St. Martha's Guest House.

As always the pope commented on the day's readings, taken from the First Letter of St. Peter (5:5-14) and Mark's gospel (16:15-20). "Before going up to heaven God sends out the apostles to preach the gospel, to preach the kingdom," he began. Then he stressed the universality of the church's mission, remarking that Jesus didn't tell the apostles to go to Jerusalem or Galilee, but to the whole world. So he opens up a wide horizon. Hence we can understand the true dimension of the "Christian mission" that goes out preaching "to the whole world." But, the pope said, "it doesn't go alone; it goes with Jesus."

So the apostles set out and preached everywhere. But "the Lord," he said, "worked together with them. The Lord works with all those who preach the gospel. This is the magnanimity that Christians must have. There can't be a timid Christian. This magnanimity belongs to the Christian vocation: ever more, ever more, ever onward."

Nevertheless, he warned, something can also occur "which isn't so Christian." At that point "how should we proceed? What is the style Jesus wants for his disciples in preaching the gospel, in this missionary work?" asked the pope. And he pointed to the reply given in the text of St. Peter, which "explains that style to us a bit: 'Beloved, clothe yourselves with humility in your dealings with one another, for God opposes the proud, but gives grace to the humble.' Preaching the gospel must have this attitude, humility, service, kindness, fraternal love."

Then the pope imagined the possible objection that might be raised by a Christian to the Lord for proposing this style: "'But Lord, we must conquer the world!'" And he showed that this attitude was mistaken. "That word 'conquer' won't do. We must preach to the world. Christians must not be like soldiers who when they win the battle make a clean sweep of everything."

At this point Pope Francis referred to a medieval text which tells how, after they had won a battle and conquered a city, the Christians lined up all the pagans between the baptistery and the sword and made them choose: water—that is baptism; or weapon—that is death. And he said: "That isn't the Christian way. The Christian way is the way of Jesus, to be humble."

The Christian, he explained, "preaches, proclaims the gospel more by his witness than his words. But a wise bishop, from Italy, said a few days ago: "Sometimes we get confused and think that our gospel preaching should be a *salus idearum* rather than a *salus animarum,* salvation of ideas, rather than salvation of souls. But how is salvation of souls achieved? By humility, by kindness. St. Thomas has a beautiful phrase about this: 'It's like walking toward that horizon that never comes to an end because it's always a horizon.' So how can we proceed with this Christian attitude? He says not to be afraid of great things. Go forward, also taking the little things into account. That is divine. There is a tension between the great and the little; do both, that's Christian. Christian mission, preaching the church's gospel, goes that way."

The confirmation of this is in Mark's gospel. The pope noted: "We can't proceed in any other way. And in the gospel, at the end, there is a beautiful phrase when it says that Jesus worked with them and 'confirmed the message by the signs that accompanied it.' When we proceed with this magnanimity and also with this humility, when we are not afraid of great things, of that horizon, but also take account of little things, like humility and daily kindness, the Lord confirms the message and we go forward. The church's triumph is the resurrection of Jesus. The cross comes before that."

Let us ask the Lord today, he concluded, "to become missionaries in the church, apostles in the church but with this spirit: great magnanimity and also great humility."

FAITH IS NOT A FRAUD

Friday, April 26, 2013
ACTS 13:26–33; JN 14:1–6

Faith is not alienation or fraud, but a real path of beauty and truth, forged by Jesus to prepare our eyes to gaze without glasses 'on the marvelous face of God' in the final place prepared for each one of us. It's an invitation not to give way to fear and to live life as a preparation for seeing better, hearing better, and loving more. This was what Pope Francis said in his homily in the Mass celebrated on Friday morning, April 26, in the chapel of St. Martha's Guest House.

Pope Francis focused his homily on the passage from John's gospel (14:1-6): "'Let not your hearts be troubled. Believe in God, believe also in me. In my Father's house there are many dwelling places. If it were not so, would I have told you that I go to prepare a place for you? And if I go to prepare a place for you, I will come again and take you to myself, so that where I am there you may be also. And you know the way to the place where I am going.'"

"These words of Jesus," said the pope, "are the most beautiful words. In a farewell moment, Jesus speaks from his heart to his disciples. He knows his disciples are sad, because they realize things are not going well." So Jesus encourages them, heartens them, reassures them, gives them hope: "'Let not your hearts be troubled!' And he begins to speak like that, like a friend, also with the attitude of a shepherd. I say: the music of these words of Jesus shows the attitude of a shepherd, as a shepherd speaks to his sheep. 'Let not your hearts be troubled. Believe in God, believe also in me.'"

When he has said these words, according to the account in John's gospel, continued the pope, "he begins to speak: of what?

Of heaven, of the final home. 'Have faith in me: I remain faithful.' It's as if that is what he said." And with the metaphor, "the figure of an engineer or architect, he tells them what he's going to do: 'I go to prepare a place for you; in my Father's house there are many dwelling-places.' And Jesus is going to prepare a place for us."

"What is this preparation?" asked the pope. "How does it happen? What is this place like? What does prepare a place mean? Renting a room up above?" Preparing a place means "preparing our capacity to enjoy, our capacity to see, feel, and understand the beauty of what awaits us, of that country toward which we are traveling."

"And the whole of Christian life," continued the pope, "is a work of Jesus, of the Holy Spirit, to prepare a place for us, prepare our eyes to see." "'But Father, I can see perfectly well! I don't need glasses!' But this is a different kind of seeing. Think of those who are suffering from a cataract and need to have an operation on the cataract. They can see, but after the operation, what do they say? 'I never thought it was possible to see as well as that, without glasses!' Our eyes, the eyes of our soul, need to be prepared to look at the wonderful face of Jesus." So it's a question of "preparing our hearing to hear the beautiful things, the beautiful words. And especially, to prepare the heart: prepare the heart to love, to love more."

"On life's road," the pope explained, "the Lord is always doing that: with trials, with consolations, with sufferings, with good things. The whole of life's road is a preparation. Sometimes the Lord has to do it quickly, as he did with the good thief: he only had a few minutes to prepare him and he did it. But normally in life it takes time: to let our hearts, eyes, hearing be prepared to arrive in that country. Because it's our country."

Pope Francis warned against losing sight of this fundamental dimension of our lives and the path of faith, and against the objections of those who don't accept the prospect of eternity: "'But Father, I went to a philosopher and he told me that all these thoughts amount to alienation, that we are alienated, that our life is here and now and we don't know anything beyond it...' Some people think like that. But Jesus tells us that isn't so and says: 'Have faith also in me. What I am telling you is the truth; I am not tricking you, I am not deceiving you.' We are on the road to that country, we children of the stock of Abraham, as St. Paul says in the first reading" (Acts of the Apostles 13:26-33).

And since Abraham's time, said the pope, "we have been on the road, with that promise of the final country. If we read the eleventh chapter of the letter to the Hebrews we will find in it the story of our predecessors, our ancestors, who went on this road toward that country and greeted it from afar. Preparing for heaven is beginning to greet it from afar." And "that's not alienation: that's the truth, which is letting Jesus prepare our hearts and eyes for such great beauty. It's the road of beauty. Also the road home."

The pope ended the homily by wishing "that the Lord may give us this strong hope" and "also give us the courage to greet this country from afar." And finally "give us the humility to let ourselves be prepared, that is, let the Lord prepare our dwelling-place, the final dwelling-place for our hearts, our eyes, and our hearing."

FOR A COMMUNITY OPEN TO THE VALUES OF THE SPIRIT

Saturday, April 27, 2013
ACTS 13:44–52; JN 14:7–14

There are those who face suffering while keeping alive the joy that is born of the Spirit—like, for example, Christians still persecuted today in so many parts of the world—and those who "use money to buy favors" and make deals, or "slander to bring others down and seek help from the powerful of this world." Or perhaps they mock those who seek to live with their own sufferings in Christian joy. This comparison was the theme of Pope Francis' homily, on Saturday, April 27, in the Mass celebrated in the chapel of St. Martha's Guest House.

The pope focused particularly on the passage from the Acts of the Apostles (13:44-52), which tells the story of the confrontation between two religious communities: that of the disciples and that of what the pope described as the "closed-minded Jews (because not all the Jews were like that)." In the disciples' community, he explained, they were carrying out Jesus' commandment: "Go out and preach"—and so they preached and nearly the whole city came out to listen to the word of the Lord. And, noted Pope Francis, a feeling of happiness spread among people, which "seemed as if it would never die." When the Jews saw this happiness "they were filled with jealousy and began to persecute." They were people who "were not bad; they were good people who had a religious attitude."

"Why did they do it?" he asked. They did it simply "because their hearts were closed, they were not open to the newness of the Holy Spirit. They thought that everything had already been said, that everything was how it should be, and so they felt they were defenders of the faith. They began to speak against the apostles, to slander them. Slander." That's an attitude which is found over and over again in the course of history; "closed groups have this attitude when they make deals with power; resolve questions 'amongst ourselves.' Like those who on the morning of the resurrection, when the soldiers came to tell them: 'We have seen this.' They told the soldiers: 'Keep it quiet! Take . . . ' and they covered it all up with money. That's precisely the attitude of such closed religiosity, which lacks the freedom to open up to the Lord." In their public lives, always "in order to defend the truth—for they think they are defending the truth," they choose "slander, gossip. They are gossiping communities, they bad-mouth others and bring them down" and they look only to themselves as if they were protected by a wall.

"On the other hand, the free community," noted the pope, "with the freedom of God and the Spirit, went forward. Even during persecutions. And the word of the Lord spread throughout the whole region. It's the nature of the Lord's community to go forward, to spread, because good is like that: it always spreads! It doesn't shut itself up. That's a hallmark, a hallmark of the church. And also for our examination of conscience: what are our communities like, religious communities, parish communities? Are they communities open to the Holy Spirit, who always leads us forward to spread the word of God or are they closed communities?"

Persecutions, the pope added, begin for religious reasons, out of jealousy, but also because of a way of talking: "the community of believers, with the freedom of the Holy Spirit, speaks with joy. The disciples were full of the joy of the Holy Spirit. They spoke with beauty, they always opened ways forward, didn't they? Whereas the closed community, which is sure of itself, the community that seeks its own safety in parleying with power, or in money, speaks with hurtful words: they insult, they condemn."

And to show the lack of love in these closed communities, Pope Francis suggested that perhaps these people "had forgotten their mother's kisses when they were little. These communities know nothing of hugs and kisses. They know about duty, getting things done, closing themselves off in apparent observance. Jesus said to them: 'You are like a tomb, a sepulcher, a beautiful whited sepulcher, but nothing else.' We think today about the church, which is so beautiful. This church that goes forward. We think of so many of our brothers who suffer for this freedom of the Spirit and they suffer persecutions now, in so many places. But in their suffering these brothers are full of the joy of the Holy Spirit. These brothers, these open, missionary communities, pray to Jesus because they know what he said and what we heard just now is true: 'Whatever you ask for in my name, I will do it.' Prayer is Jesus. Closed communities pray to the powers of the Earth to help them. And that is not a good way. Let us look to Jesus who sends us out to preach the gospel, to proclaim his name with joy, full of joy. Let us not be afraid of the joy of the Spirit. And never, ever, get mixed up in things that, in the long run, lead us to become closed within ourselves. In that confinement there is no fruitfulness or freedom of the Spirit."

BLESSED SHAME

The Pope Speaks of the Spirit in Which We Should Go to Confession

Monday, April 29, 2013
1 JN 1:5—2:2; JN 14:21–26

Confession is not like going to the "dry cleaners" to get rid of our sins, or a "torture session" where we get beaten up. In fact, confession is a meeting with Jesus and touching his tenderness with our own hand. But we must approach the sacrament without deceit or half-truths, meekly and joyfully, trusting and armed with that "blessed shame," "the virtue of the humble," which lets us recognize ourselves as sinners. Pope Francis devoted his homily to the sacrament of reconciliation in the Mass celebrated on Monday morning, April 29, in the chapel of St. Martha's Guest House.

The pope began his homily with a reflection on the First Letter of John (1:5—2:2), in which the apostle "speaks to the first Christians and speaks in a simple way: 'God is light and in him there is no darkness at all.' But 'if we say we have fellowship with him, are friends of the Lord 'while we are walking in darkness, we lie and don't do what is true.' And God requires us to worship him in spirit and in truth."

"So what does it mean," asked the pope, "to walk in darkness? For we all have dark places in our lives, even moments when everything, including our own conscience, is dark, don't we? Walking in darkness means being self-satisfied. Being convinced that we have no need of salvation. That's darkness!" And, he continued, "when we go forward along this dark way, it isn't easy to turn back. Because John goes on to say (perhaps this way of thinking made him reflect): 'If we say we have no sin, we deceive ourselves, and the truth is not in us.' Look at your sins, at our sins, we are all sinners, all of us. That's the starting point."

"But if we confess our sins," the pope explained, "he who is faithful and just will forgive us our sins and cleanse us from all unrighteousness. And he represents us, doesn't he? This Lord who is so good, so faithful, so just, so forgiving. When the Lord forgives us he does justice. Yes, he does justice first to himself, because he came to save us, and when he forgives us he does justice to himself. 'I am your Savior,' and he welcomes us. He does so in the spirit of psalm 103: 'As a father has compassion for his children, so the Lord has compassion for those who fear him,' toward those who go to him. The Lord's tenderness. He always understands us, but he also doesn't let us speak. He knows everything. 'Be quiet, go in peace,' that peace which only he can give."

This is what "happens in the sacrament of reconciliation. Often," said the Holy Father, "we think going to confession is like going to the cleaners. But Jesus in the confessional is not a dry cleaners." Confession is "a meeting with Jesus who awaits us as we are. 'But Lord, look, I'm like this.' It makes us ashamed to tell the truth: I did this, I thought that. But shame is a true Christian virtue, and also a human one. The ability to feel ashamed: I don't know whether you say it like that in Italian, but in our country we call those who can't feel ashamed *sinvergüenza.* They are 'shameless' because they are unable to feel ashamed. And being ashamed is a virtue of the humble."

Pope Francis then returned to the passage from John's letter. They are words, he said, that invite us to feel trust: "The Advocate is at our side and supports us before the Father. He supports our feeble life, our sin. He forgives us. He is our defender because he supports us. So how must we go to the Lord, just as we are, as sinners? With trust, also with joy, without deceiving ourselves. We should never deceive ourselves before God! With truth. In shame? Blessed shame, that is a virtue."

Jesus awaits each of us, he repeated, quoting Matthew's gospel (11:25-30): "'Come to me, all you that are weary and carrying heavy burdens,' including the burden of sin, 'and I will give you rest. Take my yoke upon you and learn from me, for I am gentle and humble in heart.' These are the virtues Jesus asks for: humility and gentleness."

"Humility and gentleness," the pope continued, "are the framework of a Christian life. A Christian must always behave like that, with humility and gentleness. And Jesus awaits us to forgive us. We can ask him something: isn't going to confession like going to a torture session? No! It's going to praise God, because I who am a sinner have been saved by him. And is he waiting to beat me? No, but to forgive me with tenderness. And if I do the same again tomorrow? Go back again, and again and again and again. He is always waiting for us. That tenderness of the Lord, his humility and gentleness."

Finally, the pope invited us to have faith in the words of the apostle John: "If anyone does sin, we have an advocate with the Father." And he concluded. "So we can breathe again. It's beautiful, isn't it? And if we feel ashamed? Blessed shame, for this is a virtue. May the Lord give us this grace, that courage always to go to him with the truth, because truth is light. And not with the darkness of half-truths or lies before God."

FAR FROM WORLDLINESS

Tuesday, April 30, 2013
ACTS 14:19–28; JN 14:27-31

Peace, true peace, can't be bought. It's a gift from God. A gift he gives his church. In order to get it, Christians must continue to entrust the church to God, asking him to take care of it and defend it from the attacks of the Evil One, who offers us a different peace, a worldly peace, not true peace. This was the theme of Pope Francis' reflection on the morning of Tuesday, April 30, during the Mass celebrated in the chapel of St. Martha's Guest House.

The core of the pope's reflection was the word "entrust," which appears twice in the first reading, taken from the Acts of the Apostles (14:19-28). The first time is when in Perga the apostles entrust the elders to the Lord; the second, when they return to Antioch, "where they had been entrusted to the grace of God." So apostles and elders are entrusted to the Lord. This, said the pope, "means entrusting the church to the Lord. We can guard the church, we can take care of the church, can't we? We must do that by our work. But more important is what the Lord does: he is the only one who can look the Evil One in the face and conquer him. 'The prince of this world is coming against me and he can do nothing.' If we don't want the prince of this world to get hold of the church, we must entrust it to the only one who can defeat the prince of this world."

But, asked the pope, "do we pray for the church? For the

whole church? For our brothers, whom we don't know, all over
the world?" It's the Lord's church spread all over the world. And
when "we say to the Lord in our prayers: 'Lord, watch over your
church,'" we mean that church, the Lord's church, the church
that gathers "our brothers" together. That's the prayer "we should
offer from our hearts," repeated the pope, "over and over. It's easy
for us to pray to ask for a grace from the Lord, when we need
something; and it isn't difficult to pray to thank the Lord: thank
you for … But to pray for the church, for those we don't know,
but who are our brothers and sisters, since they have received the
same baptism, and to say to the Lord, 'They are yours, they are
ours … take care of them,'" is something else. It means "entrusting the church to the Lord"; it's "a prayer to make the church
grow" but it's also an "act of faith. We can't do anything, we are
all poor servants of the church: but he's the one who can take it
forward and look after it and make it grow, make it holy, defend
it, defend it 'from the prince of this world,'" that is, from the one
who "wants the church to become more and more worldly."

"That's the greatest danger," because "when the church becomes worldly, when it has the spirit of the world in it," when it
gets that peace which is not the Lord's peace—the peace Jesus
promised us saying: "I leave you peace, I give you my peace"—
then the church becomes "weak, a defeated church, incapable of
bearing the gospel, the message of the cross, the scandal of the
cross. It can't take it forward if it's a worldly church. That's why
this prayer entrusting the church to the Lord is so important and
so powerful."

We don't make a habit, said the pope, of entrusting the church
to the Lord. So I invite you to entrust the elders, the sick, children, young people to the Lord, repeating "'Look after us Lord,
who are your church': it's yours! When we have this attitude, he
will give us, in the midst of sufferings, that peace which only he
can give. That peace which the world can't give, which can't be

bought; that peace which is a true gift of the presence of Jesus in the midst of his church," even in times of great suffering, such as "persecution," and "also lesser sufferings, such as illness or family problems." All this, concluded the pope, we should entrust to the Lord, praying: "Look after your church in her suffering, so that she may not lose faith, so that she may not lose hope." And today, he added, "I'd like to say: offering this prayer of entrusting the church will do us good and do the church good; it will give us great peace and great peace to the church; it won't relieve us of sufferings, but it will make us strong in them. So let us ask for this grace of being in the habit of entrusting the church to the Lord."

No to Slave Labor

Wednesday, May 1, 2013
Gn 1:26—2:3; Mt 13:54–58

Human beings and their dignity come first. The pope reminded us of this in his homily during the Mass celebrated on Wednesday, May 1, in the chapel of St. Martha's Guest House.

Using the occasion of the feast of St. Joseph the worker, the pope dedicated his reflection to the subject of work. He took his cue from the readings for the day, the first taken from the book of Genesis (1:26—2:3) and the second from Matthew's gospel (13:54-58), which present God as creator "who worked to create the world" and the figure of St. Joseph, the carpenter "adoptive father of Jesus," from whom "Jesus learned to work."

"Today," he said, "we bless St. Joseph as a worker: but remembering St. Joseph reminds us of God the worker, Jesus the worker.

And the subject of work is very, very, very evangelical. 'Lord,' says Adam, 'I will earn my living by working.' But there is more. For this first image of God the worker tells us that work is something more than earning one's bread: work gives us dignity. Anyone working has worth, a special dignity, personal dignity: the man and the woman who work have dignity."

So anyone not working lacks this dignity. But there are so many people "who want to work and can't." And this "is a weight on our conscience, because when society is organized in that way" and "not everybody can work, be 'anointed' with the dignity of work, that society doesn't go well. It's not just! It goes against God himself, who wants our dignity to be founded on this."

"Jesus too," continued the pope "worked hard on Earth, in Joseph's workshop. But he also worked right up to the cross. He did what the Father had commanded him to do. I think today of so many people who work and have this dignity... Let us thank the Lord! And we are aware that this dignity doesn't bring us power, money, culture, no! ... It's work that gives dignity," even if society doesn't allow all to work.

Then the pope referred to those social, political, and economic systems in various parts of the world that have based their organization upon exploitation. That is, they have chosen "not to pay fairly" and to try and get the maximum profit at any cost, profiting from the work of others, without being bothered in the least about their dignity. That "goes against God!" he exclaimed, referring to dramatic situations that occur all over the world, which *L'Osservatore Romano* has so often denounced. The pope cited the headline of an article that appeared on the front page of the edition of Sunday, April 28, about the collapse of a factory in Dacca, killing hundreds of workers who had been working in exploitative and unsafe conditions. "A headline," he commented, "that struck me hard on the day of the Bangladesh tragedy: 'How to die for 38 euros a month.' That," the pope declared plainly, "is slave labor," which exploits "the finest gift God has given to humans: the capacity to create, to work, to get our dignity from that. How many brothers and sisters in the world are in this situation because of these economic, social, and political attitudes!"

The pope then drew from the treasures of Hebrew wisdom to stress how the dignity of the human person is a universally recognized value, which must therefore be protected and maintained. "Remember," he said, "a lovely medieval Hebrew story. A rabbi was talking to his faithful about the building of the tower of Babel. At that time they built with brick. But a lot went into making the bricks, didn't it? They had to take earth, make mud, take straw, boil it. So a brick was a very precious thing. They carried each brick up to the top, to build the tower of Babel. When one brick accidentally fell down, it was a tremendous problem, a scandal: 'Look what you've done!' But if someone who was building the tower fell, all they said was 'Rest in peace!' and left him there. The brick was more important than the person! That was the story told by the medieval rabbi and it's still happening now! People are less important than things that make a profit for those who have political, social, and economic power." We have reached the point when we are no longer conscious of "this dignity of work, this dignity of the person. But today St. Joseph, Jesus, God, who all work, teach us the way to go toward dignity."

In conclusion, the pope urged us "to ask St. Joseph for the grace to be aware that it's only in work that we have dignity." And he suggested the attitude we should take toward those who have no work. Don't say: "those who don't work don't eat," but "those who don't work have lost their dignity!" And when we see someone "who doesn't work because he can't get work," we should say: "society has robbed this person of their dignity."

FOR A CHURCH THAT SAYS YES

Thursday, May 2, 2013
ACTS 15:7–21; JN 15:9–11

The church, as "a Yes community" formed by the Holy Spirit, against "the No church" which hampers the Spirit, "has a double job." That was the idea put forward by Pope Francis to those attending the morning Mass on Thursday, May 2, in the chapel of St. Martha's Guest House.

In his homily the pope focused on the church that came out of the upper room after the prayer of the apostles with Mary. A church, he noted, always driven by the Holy Spirit, which gradually spread all over the world, taking the gospel to pagans.

Commenting on the Acts of the Apostles (15:7-21) and John's gospel (15:9-11), the pope described the church's activity. "She reached out far to where they didn't believe in the proclamation of Jesus Christ because they didn't know him." She "went out to preach, driven by the Holy Spirit," who basically "acts in two ways. First he pushes," said the pope, thus creating "some problems." Then he builds "harmony within the church. This movement of the Holy Spirit is continual."

So the apostles went out and spread the faith in Jerusalem, where, the pope explained, the first problems arose, because they came up against so many different opinions. Especially those who held that they should accept everything laid down by doctors of the law. But there were also others who believed in the possibility of coming to an agreement. These were open-minded people, said the pope, but they were up against a "'No church': 'No, it can't be done; no, no, we must, we must, we must,'" in contrast to the "'Yes church': 'Yes, let's think about it, let's be open-minded, it's the Spirit opening the door to us.'" So "the Spirit had to do his second job: to create harmony between these positions, harmony in the church, between those in Jerusalem and between them and the pagans. It's fine work that the Holy Spirit always does in history. And when we don't allow him to work, divisions appear in the church, sects, all those things, because we are closed to the truth of the Spirit."

Then the pope focused on the words of James, bishop of Jerusalem. After hearing Peter say that the Lord wanted the nations to hear the word of the gospel through his mouth, and be converted "without any discrimination between us and them," James noted: "'from the beginning God wanted to choose from among the nations a people for his name. The words of the prophets agree on this,' and he makes his proposal. It's authoritative because he is the bishop of Jerusalem: 'We should not trouble those Gentiles who are turning to God.' So why 'are you putting God to the test?' Answering this question he says, let us not put God to the test 'by placing on the neck of the disciples a yoke that neither our fathers nor we have been able to bear.' And that is the key word: a yoke. When service of the Lord becomes a yoke, something heavy, the doors of the Christian community are closed: no one wants to come to the Lord. We on the other hand believe that we are saved by the grace of the Lord Jesus."

"That word yoke," admitted the pope, "comes into my heart, into my mind. But someone might think: 'So now Catholic communities, Christian communities that say "yes" don't have to do anything and just live it up?' Has this yoke, which is so heavy, any reality? Is there a yoke in the church? Yes: Jesus himself in the gospel we have just heard says: 'As the Father has loved me, so I have loved you. Remain in my love.' The first thing that Jesus says is: 'Remain in my love, be within my love, the love of my heart.' That's the first step." And the second is: "'If you keep my commandments you will remain in my love.' And this is the Christian community that says 'yes': from the proclamation of Jesus it remains in his love, and as a consequence, it fulfills the commandments and then sometimes says 'no.' But this 'no' comes from the 'yes' that has gone before it, that is, from having received 'the grace of Jesus who is love'."

And "when a Christian community lives in love, it confesses its sins, it worships the Lord, forgives offences, is kind to others and is a manifestation of love, then it feels bound to be faithful to the Lord and follow the commandments. It's a 'yes community' and when it says 'no' this follows from that first 'yes.'"

Finally, the pope urged the faithful: "Let us ask the Lord that the Holy Spirit may always help us to become a community of love: love for Jesus, who loved us so much"; "a 'yes' community which leads to obeying the commandments"; a community which always has "open doors. And defends us from the temptation to become puritans, in the etymological sense of the word, to seek a para-evangelical purity, a 'no' community. For the first thing Jesus asks from us is love, love for him; and he asks us to remain in his love."

CHALLENGING JESUS

Friday, May 3, 2013
1 COR 15:1–8; JN 14:6–14

Renaissance colors brightened the assembly of those who took part in the Mass celebrated by Pope Francis this morning, Friday, May 3, in the chapel of St. Martha's Guest House. These were the uniforms of about seventy Swiss Guards.

At the end of the Mass, the pope took the opportunity to thank the Swiss Guards "for their love and closeness to the church, and also their closeness to the pope and love for the pope. It's a most beautiful testimony of faithfulness to the church. May the Lord bless you for this service. The church loves you very much and so do I."

However, during the homily, the pope invited us to reflect on the need to pray with courage to obtain the grace to spread the faith in the world. As always, the pope used an expression that readily went to the heart and memory of his listeners and left its mark: he spoke of a brave prayer, almost like a challenge to Jesus, who said: "Whatever you ask for in my name, I will do it, so that the Father may be glorified in the Son." So praying means "having the courage to go to Jesus and ask him: 'Well that's what you said, so do it! Let the faith go ahead.'"

The pope referred to the day's readings, taken from the first letter to the Corinthians (15:1-8) and John's gospel (14:6-14). "When the apostles had decided to appoint deacons," he began, "it was because there was so much work assisting the widows and orphans" and they felt distracted from what was their duty "to proclaim the word and to pray." A task, he explained, which belongs to the ministry of bishops, but also to "all of us Christians who have received the faith: we must communicate it; we must give it; we must proclaim it by our lives, by our words. It's the transmission of the faith that goes from house to house, from family to family, from person to person."

The bishop of Rome then referred to the "beautiful text" in the letter to Timothy in which Paul speaks to him of the faith "'that you received from your mother and your grandmother and must pass on to others.' That's how we received the faith, in the family; faith in Jesus." What faith are we talking about? The faith that Paul is talking about, he explained: "'I handed on to you what I in turn had received.' He had received the faith and now gives the faith: that Christ "died for our sins in accordance with the scriptures, that he was buried, and that he was raised on the third day in accordance with the scriptures, and that he appeared to the twelve." The foundation and force of the faith are "in the Risen

Jesus, Jesus who has forgiven our sins by his death and reconciled us with the Father. Handing this on requires us to be brave: with the courage to hand on the faith. Which is sometimes simply courage."

The pope vividly evoked personal memories to make his message even clearer and anchor it in the reality of lived experience. "I remember—excuse me, this is a personal story—that every Friday my granny took us to the procession of candles, and at the end of the procession came the Christ lying down. And our granny made us kneel and said to us children: 'Look he is dead but tomorrow he will rise again!' That's how our faith began: faith in Christ who died and rose again." The pope recalled that so many people have tried to destroy "this strong certainty" and spoken of "a spiritual resurrection." But that's not it: "Christ is alive!" He died and rose again; he appeared to the apostles and made Thomas put his finger into his wounds; he ate with them. "Christ," he repeated, "is alive and still alive among us." And it's up to us to proclaim it, to proclaim the faith with courage.

But there is another kind of courage, explained the Holy Father. "Jesus, to put it strongly, challenges us to pray and says this: 'Whatever you ask for in my name, I will do it, so that the Father may be glorified in the Son. If you ask me for anything in my name I will do it.' But that's quite something! Let us have the courage to go to Jesus and ask him: 'But you said so, so do it! Make the faith go ahead, make the gospel go ahead, let this problem be solved…' Do we have this courage in prayer? Or do we pray a bit so-so, as we can, not spending much time in prayer?"

Then the bishop of Rome quoted the Old Testament, where it speaks of Abraham's courage when he asks God to save Sodom: "'But if there were forty-five just men, would you save it? And if there were forty, thirty-five…' He negotiated with God," recalled the pope. But it "requires courage" to do that. Courage is also going to the Lord to plead for others, as Moses did in the wilderness. And when the church loses this courage, "it becomes lukewarm." Lukewarm Christians who lack courage, said the pope, "do so much harm to the church," because lukewarmness closes us in on ourselves. And so problems arise between people, and they lose sight of the wider horizon. But above all, this lukewarmness affects "the courage to pray" and "the courage to proclaim the gospel."

Nevertheless, the pope noted, we all "have the courage to get caught up in our small affairs, our jealousies, our envies, in careerism, in pressing selfishly ahead … in all these things. But that does no good to the church… The church must be brave! We must all be brave in prayer, challenging Jesus: 'You said that, so do me the favor…' And we must persevere."

PERSECUTION BY THE PRINCE OF THIS WORLD

Saturday, May 4, 2013
ACTS 16:1–10; JN 15:18–21

Christians are persecuted more today than at the beginning of Christian history. The original cause of every persecution is hate by the prince of this world for those who have been saved and redeemed by Jesus through his death and resurrection. The only weapons we can defend ourselves with are the word of God, humility, and gentleness.

This morning, Saturday, May 4, Pope Francis showed a way to learn to disentangle ourselves from the snares of the world. These snares, he explained in the homily at the Mass celebrated in the chapel of St. Martha's Guest House, are works of the "devil," "the prince of this world," "the spirit of the world."

Commenting on the day's readings taken from the Acts of the Apostles (16:1-10) and John's gospel (15:18-21), the pope focused his reflection on hatred, "a strong word," he stressed, "used by Jesus. Hatred. He who is an expert in love, one who so enjoyed speaking about love, speaks of hatred." But, said the pope, "he liked calling things by their right name. And he tells us: 'Don't be afraid. The world will hate you. Know that before it hated you it hated me.' And he also reminds us of what perhaps he said on another occasion to the disciples: 'Remember what I said to you: a servant is not greater than his master. If they have persecuted me, they will also persecute you.' The Christian way is the way of Jesus." There is no other way to follow him. One of those indicated by Jesus, said the pope, "is a consequence of the world's hatred and also of the prince of this hatred in the world."

Jesus, the pope explained, has chosen us and "has rescued us. He has chosen us out of pure grace. By his death and resurrection he has rescued us from this world's power, from the devil's power, from the power of the prince of this world. The origin of hatred is this: we are saved and the prince of this world, who doesn't want us to be saved, hates us and stirs up persecutions and has done so from the time of Jesus, continuing up to this day. So many Christian communities are persecuted in the world. At this time more than in the early days. Today, now, on this very day, at this very hour. Why? Because the spirit of the world hates us."

Usually persecution occurs at the end of a long journey. We think, suggested pope Francis, "how the prince of this world tried to deceive Jesus when he was in the wilderness: 'Be clever! Are you hungry? Well, eat then. You can do it.' He also invited him to vanity: 'Be clever! You came to save people. Save time, go to the temple, throw yourself down, the people will see this miracle and it will be all over: you will have authority.' But think about this. Jesus never replied to this prince in his own words! Never. He was God. Never. For his reply he found words of God and replied in

God's words." A message for people today: "You can't parley with the prince of this world. Let that be clear."

Dialogue is something else: "it's necessary between ourselves," explained the bishop of Rome, "it's necessary for peace. Dialogue is a habit, it's an attitude we should have among ourselves in order to listen to each other and understand each other. And it must always be carried on. Dialogue is born of kindness, of love. But you can't dialogue with the prince of this world. You can only answer in the words of God, who defends us." The prince of this world, he reiterated, "hates us. And as he did with Jesus, so he will do with us: 'But look, do this… it's a small trick… it's nothing… it's a small thing' and so he begins to lead us along a road that is a bit wrong."

He begins with small things, then he starts on the flattery and so "softens us up" until "we fall into the trap. Jesus told us: 'I send you out like lambs among wolves. Be wise, be simple.' But when we let ourselves be overcome by vanity and think we can defeat the wolves by becoming wolves ourselves, 'they eat us alive.' Because if you cease to be a lamb, you have no shepherd to defend you and you fall into the power of these wolves. You might ask: 'Father, what weapon can defend us from these enticements, these pyrotechnics by the prince of this world and his flattery?' The weapon is the same one Jesus used: the word of God, and then humility and gentleness. Think of Jesus when they slapped him in the face: what humility, what gentleness! He could have insulted them but instead he only asked a humble and gentle question. Think of Jesus in his passion. The prophet says of him: 'As a sheep that is led to the slaughter he didn't open his mouth.'"

"Humility. Humility and gentleness: these are the principal weapons which the prince of this world, the spirit of this world, can't tolerate, because his proposals are of worldly power, of vanity, of wealth. He can't bear humility and gentleness." Jesus is meek and humble of heart and "today," said the pope coming to his conclusion, "he makes us think of this hatred of the prince of this world against us, against the followers of Jesus." And let us think of the weapons we have to defend ourselves with: "let us always stay as lambs because then we have a shepherd to defend us."

A Traveling Companion

Monday, May 6, 2013
ACTS 16:11–15; JN 15:26—16:4

A "friend" who is for each of us a "traveling companion" every day. That's the Holy Spirit, according to Pope Francis, who on this morning of Monday, May 6, celebrated Mass as usual in the chapel of St. Martha's Guest House. In order to know the Spirit, and especially in order to know his action in our lives, "it's important," the pope advised, "to make an examination of conscience" every night before going to sleep.

Referring to John's gospel (15:26–16:4), the pope recalled the moment when Jesus said goodbye to his disciples, assuring them "he won't leave them alone: 'I will send you the Holy Spirit.'" With this promise "the Lord goes on to explain who the Holy Spirit is, what he will do in us, the Holy Spirit. And today," said the pope, "he gives us something to think about: 'He will testify on my behalf.' The Holy Spirit really is God, God the person who testifies on behalf of Jesus Christ in us. He is the one who says: 'This is Jesus the Lord. The Lord does this. This is the way of Jesus.' And he calls him the Advocate (Paraclete), that is, the one who defends us, who is always beside us to support us."

So "Christian life," he said, "can't be understood without the presence of the Holy Spirit: it wouldn't be Christian. It would be a pious, pagan religious life," like that of someone who "believes in God but without the vitality that Jesus wants from his disciples." Moreover, he continued, "it's the Spirit who testifies on behalf of Jesus so that we can give this testimony to others."

Commenting on the first reading, taken from the Acts of the Apostles (16:11-15), the pope gave the example of Lydia, the woman who listened to Paul: "It's said of her that the Lord opened her heart to listen eagerly to what was said by Paul. That's what the Spirit does: he opens our hearts to know Jesus." He acts in us "all through the day, throughout our lives, as a witness who tells us where Jesus is."

And the best moment to discover him, according to the pope, is at the end of the day, when following a Christian habit, we make our examination of conscience. Before going to bed, the Christian "thinks about what has happened" and "what the Lord has said, what the Holy Spirit has done in me. Have I listened to the Holy Spirit? Or have I looked elsewhere? This exercise of examining our conscience does us good because it means becoming aware of what the Lord has done in our heart today, what the Holy Spirit has done." And "this helps to make the richness of Easter productive, make Easter ever present in us, as we prayed in our prayer today. Let us ask for the grace to become accustomed to the presence of this traveling companion, this witness to Jesus who tells us where Jesus is, how to find Jesus, what Jesus is telling us."

It was Jesus himself who left us the Spirit as our friend. So, reiterated the pope, it's good to keep the habit "of asking ourselves before the day has ended: 'What has the Holy Spirit done in me today? What witness has he given me? How has he spoken to me? What has he suggested to me?' He is a divine presence who helps us go forward in our Christian life." Finally, the bishop of

Rome invited everyone to ask for the grace "in every moment to keep the richness of Easter present."

JOY IN FORBEARANCE

Tuesday, May 7, 2013
ACTS 16:22–34; JN 16:5–11

Joy and the strength of Christian forbearance makes people younger and helps them to accept and patiently endure life's sufferings and difficulties. Pope Francis reminded us of this in his homily during the Mass celebrated this morning, Tuesday, May 7, in the chapel of St. Martha's Guest House.

The day's readings—taken from the Acts of the Apostles (16:22-24) and John's gospel (16:5-11)—gave the pope his cue to speak again about the spirit of endurance shown by the early Christian martyrs. He recalled the witness of Paul and Silas, who, when they were in prison, remained in prayer and singing hymns to God. The other prisoners listened to them in amazement: "Beaten and wounded 'they sing and pray...these are rather strange people!' But," said the pope, "they were at peace. They were even joyful at having suffered in the name of Jesus. They were calm. They sang, they prayed, and they suffered. At that moment they were in that very Christian state of mind: the state of patience. When Jesus starts on the road of his passion, after supper, 'he goes in patience.'"

Going in patience: that's "the way that Jesus teaches us Christians. Going in patience." But that "doesn't mean being sad. No, no, it's something else! It means enduring, bearing the weight of difficulties on your shoulders, the weight of contradictions, the weight of suffering."

Christian endurance, to which Paul and Silas bore witness, is "a process of Christian maturity," explained the pope, "along the road of patience"; because you get there but it takes time. "It's like good wine," he said with an apt expression, wine which waits patiently "for the moment when it's properly mature."

Then he recalled the example of the martyrs "who were joyful to be bearing witness to Jesus. I think, for example, of the martyrs of Nagasaki Hill: they helped one another, they gave each other strength, they spoke of Jesus awaiting the moment of his death. And it was said of some Roman martyrs that they went to their martyrdom as to a wedding, to a feast, a wedding feast." But that doesn't mean being masochistic, he said. It simply means "setting out on the way of Jesus," who was the first to enter the dimension of patience, by enduring his passion.

In the face of sufferings, we should not give way to the temptation to grumble, because "a Christian who continually grumbles" ceases to be a good Christian and becomes "Lord or Lady Grumbler." On the other hand, the good Christian discovers "silence in patience, the silence of Jesus," who during his passion only spoke "two or three necessary words." But this isn't a sad silence, just as the silence of Jesus was not sad when he endured the cross: "It's painful, sometimes very painful, but it isn't sad," because the heart is at peace.

So enduring like Jesus, with our hearts at peace, makes us happy. And the pope explained the cause of this joy by returning to the first prayer of the Mass, in which "the church says: 'Your people rejoices, Lord, in the renewed youth of Easter.' Going in patience restores our youth, it makes us younger. The patient person is the one who, in the long term, is younger! Let us think of those old people in a retirement home; those who have endured so much in their lives. Let's look into their eyes, young eyes; they have a young spirit and renewed youth. And that's what the Lord invites us to," and also "to bear with one another" in "kindness and love."

JESUS DOESN'T EXCLUDE ANYBODY

Wednesday, May 8, 2013
ACTS 17:15, 22—18:1; JN 16:12–15

Jesus didn't exclude anybody. He built bridges, not walls. His message of salvation is for everybody. This morning, Wednesday, May 8, during Mass in the chapel of St. Martha's Guest House, Pope Francis focused on the behavior of the good gospel preacher: open to all, ready to listen to all, without exception. Fortunately, he noted, "now is a good time in the church's life: these last fifty or sixty years have been a good time. For I remember when I was a child it was felt in Catholic families, in mine too: 'No we can't go to their house, because they were not married in church.' It was exclusion. No, you couldn't go! Or because they are socialists or atheists, we can't go. Now, thanks be to God, we don't hear that said."

The example given by the pope is that of the apostle Paul on the Areopagus (Acts of the Apostles 17:15, 22–18:1), where he proclaims Jesus Christ among the worshipers of idols. According to the pope it was important the way he did it: "He doesn't say: 'You idol-worshipers go to hell!'" but "tries to reach their hearts." At the beginning he doesn't condemn them but tries to have a dialogue: "Paul is a *pontifex*, a bridge-builder. He doesn't want to become a wall-builder." Building bridges to proclaim the gospel, "that's Paul's attitude in Athens: to make a bridge into their hearts, and then to take a step further and proclaim Jesus Christ."

Paul is brave and "that makes us think of the right attitude for a Christian. A Christian should proclaim Jesus Christ in a way that will get Jesus Christ accepted, received not rejected." And "the proclamation of the truth depends on the Holy Spirit. Jesus tells us in today's gospel (John 16:12-15): 'When the Spirit of truth comes he will guide you into all truth.' Paul doesn't say to the Athenians: 'This is the encyclopedia of truth. Study it and you will have the truth!'"

So truth "doesn't come in an encyclopedia"; rather, it's "a meeting with the highest truth, Jesus the great truth. No one is master of the truth" and, said the pope, it can't be managed at will, it can't be exploited, even "to defend ourselves." And again: "the apostle Paul tells us: 'You must give an account of your hope.' Yes, but it's one thing to give an account of our hope but another to say: 'We have the truth: this is it. If you don't accept it, go away.'" Paul copied the attitude of Jesus, who spoke to everyone: "He listened to the Samaritan woman, he conversed with her; he went to dinner with Pharisees, sinners, publicans, doctors of the law. Jesus listened to everybody, and when he said a word of condemnation it was at the very end, when there was nothing else to say."

But Paul is also "conscious that he must preach the gospel, not make proselytes." "The church doesn't grow by proselytism; Benedict XVI told us that. It grows by attraction, by witness, by preaching." Finally, "Paul behaves like that because he is sure, sure of Jesus Christ. He didn't doubt the Lord. Christians who are afraid to make bridges and prefer to build walls are Christians who are unsure of their own faith, unsure of Jesus Christ. And they defend themselves" by building walls.

Paul teaches us what should be the way to preach the gospel, a way we should bravely follow. And "when the church loses apostolic courage, it becomes a closed church. Tidy, neat; everything just so, but barren, because it has lost the courage to go out to those on the edges, where so many people are victims of idolatry, of worldliness, of weak thinking." And if fear of making a mistake holds us back, we need to remember that we can get up again and walk on. "Those who won't walk on for fear of making a mistake," concluded Pope Francis, "make an even bigger mistake."

Melancholy Isn't Christian

Friday, May 10, 2013
Acts 18:9–18; Jn 16:20–23

Pope Francis spoke about joy this morning, Friday, May 10, during the Mass in the chapel of St. Martha's Guest House. He ascribed his state of mind to the presence, in the same residence, of His Holiness Tawadros II, Pope of Alexandria [of the Coptic Orthodox Church]. And he wanted to share his joy with the faithful present at the Mass.

"Today," he said, "we have a great reason for joy in the House, where the Pope of Alexandria, the Patriarch of the Church of Mark, is a guest." And he explained why that was a reason for joy: "He is a brother who has come to talk to the Church of Rome, to go part of the way together. He is a brother bishop"; he "is a bishop like me and he is taking the church forward. Let us ask the Lord to bless him and help him in his ministry to take the Coptic Church forward; and also to help us to be able to go this part of the way together. This is a true joy, a joy for today. Let us thank the Lord for this joy."

The pope's reflection on joy was inspired by a passage from Luke's gospel (24:50–53), which speaks of the Lord's ascension and says that the disciples "returned to Jerusalem full of joy. The gift Jesus had given them," explained the pope, "was not a kind of nostalgia" but "it was joy." This was the joy, he said a bit later, that Christians should also cultivate and bear witness to today and not be sad. Melancholy Christians, he added, have vinegar faces "like pickled peppers."

The joy he was speaking of was the joy that Jesus had promised to his disciples: Christian joy. And he had assured them "no one can take it from you." But what is this joy? asked the pope. "Is it merriment? No, that's not the same thing. It's good to be merry, to enjoy ourselves. But joy is more than that, it's something else. It's a gift. We can't be merry all the time or it will end up becoming trivial, superficial, and it also leads us to a lack of Christian wisdom; it makes us become rather silly, naïve, doesn't it? Is everything merry? No. But joy is something else. Joy is a gift from the Lord. It fills us inside. It's like an anointing of the Spirit."

And this joy lies "in the certainty that Jesus is with us and with the Father. The other day," the pope recalled, "I said that Paul went out to preach; he built bridges because he was sure of Jesus." And that same certainty gives us joy. "The joyful man or woman is one who is sure" that Jesus is with us. But is this a certainty we can always have? A certainty "that we can bottle," said the pope in a vivid metaphor, "so that we always have it with us? No, because if we want to keep this joy just for ourselves, in the end it goes off and our heart becomes rather jaded and our face doesn't express that great joy but, instead of it, a nostalgia, a melancholy which is not healthy. Sometimes those melancholy Christians have 'faces like chili peppers in vinegar,'" rather than being joyful and happy in their lives.

But, said the Holy Father, joy can't stay still: it must go forward, because "it's a pilgrim virtue. It's a gift that goes ahead, that walks along life's road, walks like Jesus: preaching, proclaiming Jesus. Joy opens the road out further and broadens it." It's a virtue of the great, "those great souls," he said, "who are above littleness, above meanness, who don't get involved in those little internal matters that go on in a community, in the church; they always look toward the horizon."

"Joy is a virtue for the road. St. Augustine said: 'Sing and walk on!' That's Christian joy; the Christian sings with joy, and walks on, bearing this joy. Sometimes this joy may be somewhat hidden by the cross but the Christian sings and walks on. The Christian knows how to praise God, as the apostles did when they returned from the mountain after the ascension of Jesus. Joy is the gift that leads us to the virtue of magnanimity. Christians are magnanimous, they can't be pusillanimous: they are magnanimous. And magnanimity is the virtue of breathing freely; it's the virtue of always going ahead, with a spirit full of the Holy Spirit."

Two Ways Out for the Christian

Saturday, May 11, 2013
Acts 18:23–28; Jn 16:23–28

The wounds of Jesus are still present on Earth. To realize that we need to go out of ourselves and go to meet our brothers and sisters in need, the sick, the ignorant, the poor, the exploited. This is the way out—exodus—that Pope Francis pointed to for Christians in his homily during the Mass celebrated on Saturday morning, May 11, in the chapel of St. Martha's Guest House.

This means, explained the pope, "going out of ourselves," which we are enabled to do through prayer "to the Father in the name of Jesus." On the other hand, prayer that "bores us is always shut off within ourselves like a passing thought. But true prayer means going out of ourselves toward the Father in the name of Jesus; it's an 'exodus' from ourselves," which is offered "with the intercession of Jesus himself, who stands before the Father and shows him his wounds."

But how can we recognize these wounds of Jesus? How can we have confidence in these wounds, if we don't know them? And what is "the school where we learn to know the wounds of Jesus, these priestly wounds of intercession?" The pope's answer was explicit: "If we don't manage to go out of ourselves toward those wounds, we won't ever learn the freedom that leads us to the other way of going out of ourselves, toward the wounds of Jesus."

Hence the image of the two "ways out of ourselves" indicated by the Holy Father: the first "toward the wounds of Jesus, the second toward the wounds of our brothers and sisters. And that's the way Jesus wants us to follow in our prayer." These words are confirmed in John's gospel (16:23-38), in today's liturgy. It's a passage in which Jesus speaks with disarming clarity: "'Very truly, I tell you, if you ask anything of the Father in my name, he will give it to you.'" In these words, noted the pope, "something new has come into prayer: in my name." So the Father "will give us everything, but always in the name of Jesus."

What does it mean to ask in the name of Jesus? This is something new that Jesus reveals "at the very moment when he is leaving the Earth and returning to the Father." On the feast of the Ascension celebrated last Thursday, recalled the pope, there was a passage from the letter to the Hebrews, where it says among other things: "Since we have the freedom to go to the Father." This is "a new freedom. The doors are open: by going to the Father, Jesus left the door open." Not because "he forgot to shut it" but because "he himself is the door." He is "our intercessor and so he says 'in my name.'" In our prayer, characterized by "that courage which Jesus himself gives us," we ask the Father in Jesus' name: "Look at your Son and do this for me!"

The Holy Father then recalled the image of Jesus "entering the sanctuary of heaven, like a priest. Until the end of the world, Jesus is like a priest; he makes intercession for us, he intercedes for us." And when we "ask the Father saying 'Jesus,' we signal, we refer to our intercessor. He prays for us before the Father."

So, referring to the wounds of Jesus, the pope noted that Christ "in his resurrection had the most beautiful body: the wounds of the scourging, the thorns, had all disappeared. The bruises from his beating had vanished." But, added the pope, Jesus "always wanted to keep his wounds and the wounds them-

selves are his prayer of intercession to the Father." This is "the
new thing that Jesus tells us," inviting us "to have confidence in
his passion, have confidence in his victory over death, confidence
in his wounds." For indeed, he is the "priest and this is the sacrifice: his wounds." All this "gives us confidence, gives us the courage to pray," because as the apostle Peter writes, "by his wounds
you were healed."

In conclusion, the pope recalled another passage from John's
gospel: "Until now you have not asked for anything in my name.
Ask and you will receive, so that your joy may be complete."
This, he explained, refers to the "joy of Jesus," to the "joy that
is to come." This is "the new way of praying: with confidence,"
with that "courage that lets us know that Jesus is standing before the Father" and showing him his wounds; but also with the
humility to recognize and find Jesus' wounds in his brothers and
sisters in need. And that's our prayer in kindness.

So the pope hoped, "May the Lord give us this freedom to
enter into that sanctuary where he is the priest and intercedes for
us, and anything we ask from the Father in his name, he will give
us. But may he also give us the courage to go into that other 'sanctuary,' the wounds of our brothers and sisters in need, those who
suffer, who are still carrying the cross and have not yet conquered,
as Jesus has conquered."

THE HOLY SPIRIT, THE UNKNOWN

Monday, May 13, 2013
ACTS 19:1–18; JN 16:29–33

I would venture to say "the Holy Spirit, the Unknown," thinking
of so many people today who "don't know how to explain the

Holy Spirit and say, 'I don't know what to make of him,' or tell you, 'The Holy Spirit is the dove, the one who gives you seven gifts.' So the poor Holy Spirit always comes last and doesn't have much place in our lives."

Once again this morning, Monday, May 13, during his homily in the Mass celebrated in the chapel of St. Martha's Guest House, Pope Francis focused his reflection on the figure of the Holy Spirit, pointing out the scant knowledge of him that many Christians have today.

The pope took his cue from the story of Paul's meeting with some disciples in Ephesus. As we read in the Acts of the Apostles (19:1-8), when he asked them whether they had received the Holy Spirit, they replied that they had never even heard of his existence. In order to explain the episode, the Holy Father referred, as is his custom, to a moment in his personal experience. "I remember once, when I was a parish priest in the parish of the patriarch St. Joseph, in San Miguel, during a Mass for children on the day of Pentecost I asked: 'Who knows who the Holy Spirit is?' And all the children put up their hands." One of them replied: "'The Paralytic!' That's how he said it. He had heard the word 'paraclete' and had understood 'paralytic'! And that's how it is: the Holy Spirit is always somewhat unknown in our faith. Jesus tells the apostles about the Spirit: 'I will send you the Holy Spirit: he will teach you all things and will remind you of everything that I have said.' Let's think about that: the Holy Spirit is God, but he is God active in us, making us remember. God who awakens our memory. The Holy Spirit helps us to keep memory alive."

And "it's so important to keep memory alive," repeated the pope, because "a Christian with no memory is not a true Christian, but a man or a woman" who is a prisoner of the moment, who has no history. They do have a history but they don't know how to treasure it. The Holy Spirit teaches us that. Memory which "comes from the heart," said the pope, "is a grace of the Holy Spirit." And so is even the memory "of our miseries and our sins," "the memory of our enslavement: sin makes us slaves. To remember our history, and how the Lord has saved us, is a beautiful thing. And that impelled Paul to say: 'But my sins are my glory. But I do not boast of them: it's the only glory I have. But by his cross he has saved me.'"

Memory does us good, even when it's an attack of vanity "and thinks it's a sort of Nobel Prize of holiness," said the pope. Memory does us good "but remember where it has taken you from: from the back of the flock. You were the last in the flock." Memory is a great grace, "and the church also has her memory, the Lord's passion," that memory which takes away sin. "Today," said the Holy Father, "I'd like to ask for the grace of that memory for all of us," to ask "the Holy Spirit to make us all 'mindful,' that is to say, 'mindful' men and women." This intention was commended to the Virgin Mary, "lady of memory."

At the end of the Mass Pope Francis gave a "parish notice," as he put it himself, and wished a happy birthday to Mgr. Peter Bryan Wells, Assessor at the Secretariat of State, who was present at the Mass together with his father and brother. The pope thanked him "for everything you have done for the good of the church."

SATAN ALWAYS SWINDLES US

Tuesday, May 14, 2013
ACTS 1:15–17, 20–26; JN 15:9–17

Selfishness gets us nowhere. But love frees us. So anyone who is able to live life as "a gift to others" will never be lonely and won't suffer "the drama of an isolated consciousness" that falls easy prey to "Satan the bad payer," who is ever "ready to swindle" those who choose his way. That was the reflection offered by Pope Francis this morning, Tuesday, May 14, to those present at the Mass celebrated in the chapel of St. Martha's Guest House.

Commenting on the readings for the day, taken from the Acts of the Apostles (1:15-17, 20-26) and John's gospel (15:9-17), the pope began by saying that at this time of waiting for the Holy Spirit the idea of love returns, the new commandment. "Jesus gives us a strong message: 'No one has greater love than this: to lay down your life for your friends.' The greatest love: to lay down your life. Love always goes that way: giving your life. To live life as a gift, a gift to give. It isn't a treasure to hang on to. And that's how Jesus lived, as a gift. And if we live our lives as a gift, we are doing what Jesus wants: 'And I appointed you to go and bear fruit.'" So we should not consume our lives in selfishness.

The pope returned to the figure of Judas, whose attitude is against love, because "the poor man never understood what a gift is." Judas was one of those men who never do an unselfish deed and who always live enclosed in their own ego without "ever being carried away by beautiful occasions." Not like "Mary Magdalene, who was, when she bathed Jesus' feet in costly spikenard ointment."

That, said the bishop of Rome, "was a religious moment, a moment of gratitude, and a moment of love." Judas, on the other hand, lives detached. He goes on his way along his lonely road. "Bitterness of heart," said the Holy Father. And just as "love increases in giving," so too the other attitude of "selfishness grows. And it grew in Judas until he finally betrayed Jesus." Anyone who loves, said the pope, gives their life as a gift; anyone who is selfish betrays, remains always alone and "isolates their consciousness in selfishness, in taking care of their own life but then in the end losing it."

And it's easy for all of us to fall into selfishness. Once again the pope pointed to the example of Judas, who "was an idolater, worshiping money. John tells us he was a thief. And that idolatry led him to become isolated from the community of other people: that is the drama of an isolated consciousness." When Christians begin to become isolated, "they isolate their consciousness from the sense of the community, the sense of the church, from that love which Jesus gives us." And in the end, like Judas, they lose their lives. "John tells us," said the pope recalling the gospel story, "'at that moment Satan entered into Judas' heart.' And we have to say that Satan is a bad payer. He always swindles us—always!"

So there are two ways to choose from: life for ourselves or living life as a gift. That's "what Jesus did: 'As the Father has loved me, so he sends me out of love and I give myself for love.'" In these days of waiting for the Holy Spirit, the pope concluded, "let us pray: Come, come and give me a large heart, capable of loving with humility and gentleness." And "let us also pray that he may always free us from the other way, the way of selfishness, which comes to a bad end."

When Shepherds Become Wolves

Wednesday, May 15, 2013
Acts 20:28–38; Jn 17:11–19

Bishops and priests who fall into the temptation of money and the vanity of careerism turn from shepherds into wolves, "who eat the flesh of their own sheep." Pope Francis didn't mince his words in denouncing the behavior of those, he said, quoting Augustine, "who take the sheep's meat to eat it; who profit from it, do business with it, and are attached to money, becoming greedy and sometimes even guilty of simony. Or they use the wool for their own vanity, to show off."

In order to overcome these "real and specific temptations," bishops and priests must pray, but they also need the prayers of the faithful, which the pope himself asked for this morning, Wednesday, May 15, from those attending the Mass in the chapel of St. Martha's Guest House.

The Holy Father commented on the readings of the day: the first reading (Acts of the Apostles 20:28-38) "is one of the finest pages of the New Testament," he said. It tells us about the relationship between Paul and the believers of Ephesus, that is, the relationship between the bishop and his people "consisting of love and tenderness." This relationship is also spoken about in the Gospel of John (17:11-19), "where there are some key words," the pope explained, spoken by the Lord to the disciples: "watch"; "guard, guard the people"; "build up, defend." And "Jesus says to the Father: 'sanctify.'" These are words expressing a protective relationship, a loving relationship between God and the shepherd and between the shepherd and the people. "This," said the pope, "is a message for us bishops and priests. Jesus tells us: 'Watch over yourselves and every creature.' Bishops and priests must watch, keep watch over their people. They must also look after their people, make their people grow. They must also stand guard to warn them when wolves are coming."

All this "points to a very important relationship between bishop, priest, and the people of God. For a bishop isn't a bishop for his own sake but for the people's sake; and a priest isn't a priest for his own sake but for the people's sake." This is a "very beautiful" relationship based on mutual love. And "thus the church becomes a union." You, he asked the faithful "do always think of bishops and priests, don't you? We need your prayers."

Besides, he said, the relationship between bishops, priests, and the people of God isn't based upon social concern, whereby "bishop and priest stand with the people: we here and you there." Rather, it's an "existential relationship," it's "sacramental" like that described in the gospel, in which "bishop, priest, and people kneel down and pray and weep. And that's the church united! Mutual love between bishop, priest, and people. We need your prayers to do this, because even a bishop or a priest can be tempted."

So the first job of a bishop or priest is "to pray and preach the gospel. A bishop, a priest must pray and pray often… He must proclaim Jesus Christ, risen from the dead, and proclaim him often. We must ask the Lord to guard us bishops and priests, so that we can pray, intercede, bravely proclaim the message of salvation. The Lord has saved you! And he is alive among us!"

But "we too," he added, "are human and we are sinners": we can all be sinners "and we are also tempted. What are the temptations of the bishop or priest? Commenting on the prophet Ezekiel, St. Augustine speaks of two temptations: wealth, which can become avarice, and vanity. He says: 'When the bishop or priest takes advantage of the sheep for his own sake, things change: the priest, the bishop isn't for the people but a priest or bishop who takes from the people.'" Greed and vanity: these are the two temptations St. Augustine speaks of. "It's true. When a priest or bishop goes after money, the people don't love him and that's a sign. And he himself ends badly. Paul speaks about this: 'I worked with my own hands.' Paul didn't have a bank account, he worked. And when a bishop or priest goes the way of vanity, or becomes a careerist, he does great harm to the church." And in the end he even becomes ridiculous, because "he boasts, he likes to be seen, in all his glory. And the people don't like that! So you see what our difficulty is, and also our temptations. So you must pray for us, for us to be poor, for us to be humble, gentle, and to serve the people."

The pope invited those present to re-read that page of the gospel to convince themselves of the need to pray "for us bishops and for priests. We need that so much, in order to remain faithful, to be men who watch over the flock and also over ourselves." And also pray "that the Lord may defend us from temptations, because if we go the way of riches, if we go the way of vanity, we become wolves, not shepherds."

THE PAINS OF ST. PAUL

Thursday, May 16, 2013
ACTS 22:30; 26:6–11; JN 17:20–26

By their testimony to the truth, Christians should "bother our comfortable structures," even at the expense of ending up "in trouble." Driven by a "sane spiritual madness" to "life's furthest outposts." Following the example of St. Paul, who went "from one battle to another," believers should not "take refuge in a quiet life" or in compromise. In the church today there are too many "good-mannered armchair Christians," who are "lukewarm," for whom "everything is all right" always, but who have no apostolic fire in their bellies. This was a strong call to mission—not only in faraway lands but here in the city—proclaimed by Pope Francis this morning, Thursday, May 16, during the Mass celebrated in the chapel of St. Martha's Guest House.

The starting point of his reflection was a passage from the Acts of the Apostles (22:30; 23:6-11), which shows the protagonist St. Paul in one of his "battles." But this time, said the pope, it was a battle "started partly by him, by his cunning. When he became aware of the division between those who were accusing him," between Sadducees and Pharisees, he pushed them to turn "against one another. But Paul's whole life went from one battle to another, from persecution to persecution. A life with so many trials, because the Lord himself had told him this would be his destiny"; a destiny "with so many crosses, but he keeps on going; he looks to the Lord and keeps on going."

And Paul "bothers people: he's a man," explained the pope, "who by his preaching, by his work, by his behavior, bothers people because he proclaims Jesus Christ. And the proclamation of Jesus Christ in our comfortable lives, our comfortable structures, bothers even us Christians. The Lord always wants us to go on forward, on and on." He wants us "not to take refuge in a quiet life and fragile structures. Preaching the Lord, Paul gave trouble. But that was because he had such a Christian attitude of apostolic zeal. Indeed, he had apostolic fervor. He was not a man to compromise. No! On with the truth! On with the proclamation of Jesus Christ! But this was not just because of his temperament, though he was a fiery man." Returning to the story in Acts, the pope showed how "even the Lord gets involved" in the events, because "just after this battle, on the following night he says to Paul: 'Courage! Go ahead, go on!' It's the Lord himself who presses him to go on: 'For just as you have testified for me in Jerusalem, so you must bear witness also in Rome.'" And, added the pope, "by the way, I'm pleased that the Lord should concern himself with this diocese from that early time: we are privileged!"

"Apostolic zeal," he said, "isn't an eagerness for power, it isn't trying to get anything. It's something that comes from within, which the Lord himself wants from us: to be Christians with apostolic zeal. And where does this apostolic zeal come from? It comes from the knowledge of Jesus Christ. Paul had found Jesus Christ, had encountered Jesus Christ, but not by intellectual, scientific knowledge—this is important because it helps us—but with a knowledge that comes before that, heart knowledge, by a personal encounter. The knowledge of Jesus, who has saved me and who died for me: that's the deepest point of Paul's knowledge. And that drives him forward, proclaiming Jesus."

So that's why for Paul "one thing isn't over before he begins another. He is always in trouble, not trouble for trouble's sake, but for Jesus' sake: these are the consequences of proclaiming Jesus! His knowledge of Jesus Christ makes him become a man with that apostolic fervor. He is in this church and thinks about it, he goes into another, and then goes back to the former and back to the latter. And this is a grace. It's a Christian attitude, apostolic fervor, apostolic zeal."

Then Pope Francis referred to the Spiritual Exercises of St. Ignatius Loyola, suggesting the question: "But if Christ did that for me, what must I do for Christ?" And he replied: "Apostolic fervor, apostolic zeal, can only be understood in an atmosphere of love: it can't be understood without love, because apostolic zeal has something mad about it, but a spiritual madness, a sane madness."

"The one who guards apostolic zeal," the pope continued, "is the Holy Spirit; the one who makes apostolic zeal grow is the Holy Spirit; he gives us that inner fire to go forward proclaiming Jesus Christ. We must ask him for the grace of apostolic zeal." And that is true "not only for missionaries, who do such great work. I have met some recently: 'Ah, Father, I have been a missionary in the Amazon for sixty years.' Sixty years and counting...! There are so many of these in the church now and so full of zeal: men and women who go ahead, who have this fervor. But in the church there are also lukewarm Christians. They have a certain half-heartedness, they don't feel like going ahead, they are all right. There are also armchair Christians. Those good-mannered people, all very well, but they are incapable of giving children to the church by proclaiming the gospel with apostolic fervor."So the pope called upon the Holy Spirit "to give all of us this apostolic fervor; also to give us the grace to make trouble about things that are too quiet in the church; the grace to go ahead toward life's furthest reaches. The church needs that so much! Not only in faraway lands, young churches, among peoples who still don't know Jesus Christ. But here in the city, in our own city, people need that proclamation of Jesus Christ. So let us ask the Holy Spirit for this grace of apostolic zeal, to be Christians with apostolic zeal. And if we cause trouble, blessed be the Lord. Go ahead, as the Lord says to St. Paul: 'Courage!'"

PETER'S SHAME

Friday, May 17, 2013
ACTS 25:13–21; JN 21:15–19

Being a sinner isn't a problem; but what is a problem is not repenting for having sinned, not feeling ashamed of what we have done. In his homily at the Mass this morning, Friday, May 17, at St. Martha's Guest House, Pope Francis revisited the story of the meetings between Peter and Jesus, giving them a particular reading. Jesus, he noted, "entrusts his flock to a sinner," to Peter. "A sinner but not corrupt," he immediately made clear, as if he wanted to give greater emphasis to what he was about to say, addressing those taking part in the celebration: "Sinners, yes, all of us, but not corrupt!"

The pope developed this reflection by commenting on the

readings for the day (Acts of the Apostles 25:13-21 and John 21:15-19). In particular, he highlighted the dialogue between Jesus and Peter after their first meeting "when his brother Andrew," recalled the pope, "brought him to Jesus." When Jesus has looked at him, "he says: But are you Simon? From now on I'll call you Cephas, Rock (Greek: *petra*)." It was the beginning of a mission, the pope explained, even though "Peter hadn't understood a thing, but a mission it was."

Then Pope Francis recalled the other meetings between them, which the gospel tells us about, as for example "that time when Jesus performs the miraculous catch of fishes; when Peter says to Jesus, at one meeting: I am a sinner. He also says: Depart from me, Lord, for I am a sinner! Then at another meeting with Jesus when Jesus speaks of the Eucharist, remember? Eating bread, his body—and some withdrew from him because they didn't understand," and it was a saying "they didn't like." And Jesus asks those who remain: "And do you also want to go away? And Peter says: But Lord, only you have the words of eternal life."

Then the Holy Father recalled the gospel episode of Peter's denial, when Jesus and the first of the apostles look at each other. "That look of Jesus, such a beautiful look, so beautiful! And Peter bursts into tears." This "is the story of the meetings between them," during which Jesus shapes the apostle's soul by love. That love which makes Peter weep when Jesus "asks him three times at another meeting: Simon, son of John, do you love me?" Every time Jesus repeats the question Peter remembers that he denied him; he said he didn't know him, "and he feels ashamed. That's Peter's shame, isn't it?"

In short, "he's a great man, this Peter. Sinner, sinner. But the Lord makes him feel, and makes us feel too, that we are all sinners" and "the problem isn't being sinners" but rather "not repenting of our sins, not feeling ashamed of what we have done. That's the problem. But Peter feels that shame, that humility, doesn't he?"

Peter had a great heart and this "leads him to a new encounter with Jesus, to the joy of forgiveness, that evening, when he wept." The Lord doesn't go back on what he has promised, which was "You are Rock," and at this moment he also says to him: "Feed my flock." He entrusts his flock to a sinner. "Peter," said the bishop of Rome, "was a sinner, but not corrupt, was he? Sinners yes, all of us, but not corrupt!"

Then, as often happens in these morning celebrations, Pope Francis told a story from his own life: "Once I knew about a priest, a good parish priest who did his work well. He was appointed bishop and was ashamed because he didn't feel worthy; he was in spiritual torment. He went to confession. His confessor listened to him and then said to him: But don't be afraid. If Peter who did such a great wrong was made pope, you go ahead! The Lord is like that. The Lord is like that. The Lord makes us grow up through many meetings with him, and also meeting with our weaknesses, when we recognize them, meeting with our sins. He is like that, and the story of this man who let himself be modeled—I think it can be put like that—by so many meetings with Jesus, is an example to us all, because we are on the same road, following Jesus to practice the gospel. Peter is a great man but not because he has a doctorate in this or that, or a clever man who has done this or that. No, he is a great man, a noble man; he has a noble heart, and this nobility is what makes him weep, gives him pain, shame, but also enables him to take up his work to shepherd the flock."

And so this man is an example for all of us, this man who is always meeting with the Lord, who "purifies him, makes him grow up" through these very meetings, said Pope Francis. He concluded: "Let us ask that he may help us to go ahead and seek the Lord and meet him. But even more important is for us to allow the Lord to meet us: he is always near, he's always close to us. But so often we are looking elsewhere, because we don't feel like talking with the Lord or letting the Lord meet us: that is a grace. That's the grace that Peter teaches us."

GOOD MANNERS AND BAD HABITS

Saturday, May 18, 2013
ACTS 28:16–20, 30–31; JN 21:20–25

After "armchair Christians" the pope turned again to "gossiping Christians," who may lose a proper sense of belonging to the church, to the people of God.

This morning, Saturday, May 18, during the morning celebration in the chapel of St. Martha's Guest House, Pope Francis stressed the "bad habits," as opposed to the "good manners," displayed by so many Christians. And among these bad habits is the habit of "tearing each other to pieces" with words, disinformation, and slander. "Gossips," he said, "are destructive in the church." Yes, Jesus spoke a lot with Peter and all the others, just as the apostles spoke among themselves and with the others; but it was "a loving conversation."

Jesus, the pope recalled in his homily, asked Peter several times "whether he loved him. Peter said yes and the Lord gave him a mission: Feed my flock." This was "indeed a loving conversation." But up to a point, the Holy Father explained, Peter was tempted to interfere in the life of another, Judas. Peter asked Jesus why, when he knew Judas would betray him, he allowed him to go on following him. "On another occasion Jesus had to rebuke him: 'What is that to you?' Those are strong words: 'What is that to you?' Don't interfere in someone else's life. What does it matter to you if I want this?" repeated the pope, referring to the gospel passage from John (21:20-25).

Peter, explained the bishop of Rome, is a man and so he also suffers from the temptation to interfere in other people's lives, that is, "as we say, to be a nosy parker." This also happens in our Christian lives. "How often," asked Pope Francis, "are we tempted to do this? The conversation, that conversation with Jesus went off the rails. And there are so many ways of interfering in other people's lives." The pope pointed out two: comparing ourselv es with others and gossip.

When making comparisons, he said, we always wonder: "Why does this happen to me and not to him? God isn't fair!" To make the idea clearer he gave the example of little St. Teresa, who "when she as a child was curious to understand why Jesus seemed unjust: he gave so much to one person and so little to another. She was a child and she asked her older sister. What a wise sister! She took a thimble and a glass. She filled them both with water. Then she asked: 'Tell me, Teresa, which of these two is the fullest?' 'But they are both full!' And that's how Jesus is with us. It doesn't matter whether you are great or small. What matters is whether you are full of the love of Jesus and the grace of Jesus! That's how Jesus is with us."

But when we make comparisons "we end up feeling bitter and envious. That's just what the devil wants. We begin by praising Jesus and then, by way of these comparisons, we end up feeling bitter and envious." Envy "corrodes the Christian community" and "does so much harm, so much harm to the Christian community."

The second way referred to by the Holy Father is gossip. We begin politely, "I don't want to speak ill of anyone but it seems to me that..." and we end up "tearing our neighbor to pieces. Yes, that's what we do! How much gossip there is in the church! How much we Christians gossip!" And gossip is indeed "tearing each other to pieces, wounding one another." As if we wanted to make the other person look small to make ourselves look great. For the pope this "won't do! Gossiping seems delicious. I don't know why but it seems delicious. Like honey sweets, doesn't it? You take one and you say: yum yum! And then you take another, another, another, and in the end you get a belly ache." Gossiping is like that: "it's delicious at the beginning and then it makes you sick, makes your soul sick! Gossip is destructive in the church, destructive. And then the spirit of Cain: to murder your brother, with your tongue." And we do it "with good manners. But that way we become Christians with good manners and bad habits! Christians who are polite but nasty!"

The Holy Father listed three negative ways of behaving. First of all, disinformation, when we say "only the half-truth that suits us and not the other half; we don't tell the other half because it doesn't suit us." Then there is defamation: when "someone really has a fault, we make a big thing of it"; we have to blab all about it, "act the journalist, don't we? And that person's reputation is ruined!" And third, there is slander: "saying things that are not true. That's really killing our brother!"

Disinformation, defamation, and slander "are sinful! They are sins! This is giving Jesus a slap in the face," through his children, his brothers and sisters. And "the Lord knows this, because he knows us as we are." That's why "he says to Peter: What is that to you? You, follow me! He points out the way: looking neither to right nor to left." Comparison with others "won't do you any good, but it will lead you to envy and bitterness. Follow me! Gossip won't do you good, because it will lead into this spirit of destroying the church. Follow me! That's a fine word Jesus says, very clear, very loving toward us." It's as if he said to us: don't daydream "thinking that salvation lies in comparing yourself with others or in gossip. Salvation lies in following me. Following Jesus! Today let us ask the Lord to give us this grace never to interfere in the lives of others, not to become Christians with good manners and bad habits."

Prayer Works Miracles

Monday, May 20, 2013
Sir 1:1–10; Mk 9:14–29

There are still miracles today. But to allow the Lord to work them, brave prayer is needed, prayer that is able to overcome "that hint of disbelief" which is present in every human heart, even in Christians. Above all, prayer for those who suffer from war, persecution, and all the other woes that inflict society today. But prayer must "set us alight," that is, involve our whole self and engage our whole life in overcoming disbelief. That was Pope Francis' recommendation to those taking part in the Mass celebrated this morning, Monday, May 20, in the chapel of St. Martha's Guest House.

In his homily the pope reflected on disbelief in the light of Mark's gospel story (9:14-29) of the boy possessed by an evil spirit who was freed by Christ. "This was not the first time," said the Holy Father, "that Jesus complained about disbelief: O faithless generation! He said so many times"; and he suffered greatly from this disbelief in his words, his message. "They liked him. The crowd went out to greet him. They liked him but up to a certain point. They didn't risk much in their faith with regard to him. They didn't take any risks. And Jesus suffered from this, didn't he? Those are strong words he says today: O faithless generation, how much longer must I be among you? How much longer must I put up with you?"

The pope then noted that Jesus was serious in his rebuke. So he turns firmly to the disciples and asks them to bring the boy to him. "He takes things in hand," and when "Jesus takes things in hand, they go well." But how to get the Lord to take things in hand? Of course it isn't easy, because of this disbelief. "But why disbelief?" asked the pope. "They all saw that Jesus worked miracles, so many great things. Jesus' words were so fine and they struck the heart." And it's a question of heart: "I believe," said the bishop of Rome, "that it's the heart that won't open, the closed heart, the heart that wants to keep everything under its own control." We are "afraid of failing." The pope recalled what had happened on the Sunday of the resurrection "when Jesus stood among his disciples in the upper room. Luke says: Their joy was so great that they couldn't believe it. They were afraid that this joy was a dream, a fantasy, that it wasn't Jesus…"

Returning to the episode in the gospel, the Holy Father repeated the disciples' question when they had not succeeded in driving out the evil spirit from the boy: "But why couldn't we drive it out? This kind of spirit, Jesus explains, can only be driven out by prayer." And the boy's father said: "'Lord, I believe, help my unbelief.'" That was "a strong prayer; and such a strong and humble prayer enabled Jesus to work the miracle. Prayer asking for an extraordinary action," explained the pope, "must be a prayer involving all of us, engaging all our lives. Prayer needs to set us alight."

Then the pope described something that happened in Argentina. "I remember something that happened three years ago in the sanctuary of Luján." A little girl of seven was ill, but the doctors couldn't help. She was getting worse and worse until one evening the doctors said there was nothing else to be done and she only had a few hours to live. "Her father, who was an electrician, a believer, went crazy. And driven by that madness, he jumped on the bus and went to the sanctuary of Luján, a two-and-a-half-hour journey, seventy kilometers away. He arrived at nine in the evening and found everything was shut. And he began to pray with his hands grasping the iron gate. He prayed and wept. He stayed there like that all night. That man was fighting with God. He was fighting with God himself to cure his little girl. Then at seven in the morning he went to the terminal and caught the bus. He arrived at the hospital at about nine o'clock. He found his wife crying and feared the worst. What has happened? I don't understand. What has happened? His wife answered, the doctors came and told me that the fever had gone, she is breathing well, she is all right...They are keeping her just for another two days. But they don't understand what happened. And that," said the pope, "still happens. Miracles still happen. But prayer is important! Brave prayer, which fights for the miracle, not polite prayers like: Oh, I'll pray for you! Then one Our Father, one Hail Mary and forget all about it. No! What is needed is brave prayer, like Abraham's, who fought with the Lord to save the city; like Moses, who prayed with raised hands and grew tired beseeching the Lord; like so many people who have faith and with it they pray and pray."

Prayer works miracles, but, the pope concluded, "we must believe in it. I think that we can pray a good prayer, not just a polite prayer but prayer with the heart and say all day long: Lord, I believe. Help my unbelief. We all have some disbelief in our hearts. Let us say to the Lord: I believe, I believe! You can! Help my unbelief. And when we are asked to pray for so many people who are suffering in wars, as refugees, and all these things, let us pray, but from the heart, and let us say: Lord, I am weak. I believe, Lord. Help my unbelief."

True Power Is Service

Prayer for the Victims of the Oklahoma Tornado

Tuesday, May 21, 2013
Sir 2:1–11; Mk 9:30–37

True prayer is service. This was an idea Pope Francis had already expressed on other occasions and to which he returned this morning, Tuesday, May 21, during the Mass in the chapel of St. Martha's Guest House. He was commenting on the gospel passage from Mark (9:30-37), which had been read during the liturgy. The tragic news from the United States—where a violent tornado had devastated Oklahoma City—was recalled during the prayer of the faithful, which the pope concluded by praying for the victims of the disaster.

In the gospel story Jesus is going through Galilee, together with his disciples, and speaks to them about his passion: "The Son of Man is to be betrayed into human hands and they will kill him," but after three days he will rise again. "He is speaking to his disciples," the Holy Father explained, "about this reality, about what he has to do, his service, his passion. But they did not understand his words. They were on another track and were arguing among themselves. And the Lord knew it." So when they reached Capernaum, "he asked them: What were you arguing about on the way?" And they "were silent" from shame. For on the way they had been arguing about who was the greatest among them.

Commenting on the episode, the pope said, "The struggle for power in the church isn't just something that happens today, then, is it? It began back then, when they were with Jesus." While the Lord was speaking about his passion, the disciples were arguing about who was the most important among them, who deserved "the biggest slice" of what the pope compared to a cake being cut. But it shouldn't be like that in the church. The Holy Father stressed this, quoting another gospel passage, from Matthew (20:25-26), in which Jesus explains to the disciples the true meaning of power: "The rulers of the Gentiles lord it over them, and their great ones are tyrants over them. But it must not be so among you," said the bishop of Rome. So according to the gospel, "the struggle for power in the church shouldn't exist. Or if we like, it should be a struggle for true power, which Jesus taught by his example: the power of service. True power is service. As he himself behaved, who didn't come to be served but to serve. And his service led to the cross: he humbled himself even to death, death on a cross, for us; to serve us, to save us."

In the church there is no other way to get ahead. "For the Christian," said the pope, "getting ahead, progressing, means lowering yourself. If we don't learn this Christian rule, we will never be able to understand the true Christian message about power." And "in the church the greatest is the one who serves most, who is most at the service of others. That's the rule. But from that time to this, power struggles" have always gone on in the church.

Then the pope focused on the language used to describe progress in a career: "When someone gets a job, which in the eyes of the world is a top job, we say: Oh, that woman has been promoted to president of this association and that man has been promoted." Promote. "Yes," he said, "it's a fine verb. And it should be used in the church. Yes, he has been promoted to the cross; she has been promoted to humiliation. That's true promotion. Promotion that makes us more like Jesus." In his Spiritual Exercises, St. Ignatius "tells us to ask the crucified Lord for the grace of humiliation: Lord, I want to be humiliated, to become more like you. That's love, that is the power of service in the church. And that's the way to serve others better who are on the way of Jesus," said the pope.

Other sorts of promotion have nothing to do with Jesus. These promotions the pope called "worldly," and they have existed since the time of Jesus himself. "In the church there have always been networks," he repeated, "to get on, get ahead: careerism, social climbers, nepotism." Then the pope referred to a sort of "good-mannered simony," which is secretly paying someone purely in order to get a position. "But this is not the Lord's way. The Lord's way is his service. As he served, we too should walk behind him along the way of service. That's true power in the church. Today I'd like to pray for all of us, for the Lord to give us grace to understand that true power in the church is service and also to understand that golden rule that he taught us through his example: for a Christian progress, getting ahead, means lowering yourself," he concluded.

No One Should Kill in God's Name

Wednesday, May 22, 2013
Sir 4:11–19; Mk 9:38–40

No one should kill in God's name. Even to say this is a blasphemy. Rather, everyone not only can, but must do good, whatever faith they profess, because "they have within them the commandment to do good," since they are "created in God's image." That, briefly, was the reflection offered by Pope Francis this morning, Wednesday, May 22, to those taking part in the morning Mass in the chapel of St. Martha's Guest House.

The gospel passage from Mark (9:38-40) read during the Mass refers to the disciples' complaint about someone who was doing good but who did not belong to their group. "Jesus corrects them. Don't stop him, let him do good. Thoughtlessly, the disciples wanted to lock into an idea: only we can do good, because we have the truth. And all those who don't have the truth can't do good," explained the pope.

But this attitude is wrong. And Jesus corrects it. Is it right "for us to ask ourselves: who can do good and for what reason? What does Jesus mean by saying: 'Don't stop him'? What is behind it?" Here "the disciples were a bit intolerant," but "Jesus broadens their horizon and we may well think that he is saying: If this person can do good, everyone can do good. Even those who are not with us."

But what is at the root of this capacity belonging to all? "I think it lies in the creation," replied the pope: "The Lord created us in his image," and "if he does good, we all have this commandment in our hearts: Do good and don't do evil. All of us." But to "those who say: But Father, this person isn't a Catholic, he can't do good, we reply, Yes, he can, yes, he must; he not only can but must, because he has this commandment inside him," in his heart.

Thinking that not everyone can do good is a kind of lock-out, "a wall," stressed the Holy Father, "that leads us to war" and "and to what some have done in history: killing in God's name. We can't kill in God's name." Indeed, "saying we can kill in God's name is blasphemy." The Lord has redeemed us all with Christ's blood, "all of us, not just Catholics. All of us," the bishop of Rome reminded us. And what about atheists? "Them too, all of us. It's that blood which makes us become God's children." That's why "we all have a duty to do good."

This is also "the right way toward peace." For if everyone does their part in doing good, good toward others, "we meet by doing good." And thus we build "a culture of meeting; we need it so much." So no one is left out, neither atheists nor those who think differently: "We meet by doing good," since "on this road of life" the Lord "will speak to each of us in our hearts." Doing good "is a duty, an identity card which our Father has given to all of us, because he has made us in his image and likeness. And he always does good," said the pope.

"I'd like to ask the Lord today," he concluded, "for this grace for us all. To discover the commandment we all have: do good, not evil, and work together on meeting each other in doing good." That's a way everyone can go, stressed the pope, recalling that "today is St. Rita's day, the patron saint of impossible causes"; and so if this seems impossible, "let us ask her for this grace" for us all to do good as if we were one single family. A "work of creation," he defined it, work that brings us close "to the Father's creation."

THE SALT THAT GIVES FLAVOR

Thursday, May 23, 2013
SIR 6:5–17; MK 10:1–12

The day's gospel (Mark 9:41-50) inspired the Holy Father to reflect on a characteristic peculiar to Christians: to be for the world what salt is for the housewife and for those who have good taste and appreciate the flavor of things. "Salt is good," the pope began. A good thing "that the Lord created," but "if the salt becomes insipid," he asked, "how can you make things tasty?"

He was speaking of the salt of faith, hope, and love. "The Lord gives us this salt," said the Holy Father and then raised the problem of how to ensure that "it doesn't become insipid." "How can we make sure the salt doesn't lose its taste?" The taste of Christian salt, he explained, comes from the certainty of faith, hope, and love given by the awareness that "Jesus rose again for us" and "has saved us." But that certainty hasn't been given to us merely to hoard it. If that were so, it would be like salt stored in a jar: "it doesn't do anything, it doesn't work." But, said the pope, salt makes sense when it's used to flavor things. I think salt stored in a jar can lose its strength through humidity. And it doesn't work. The salt we have received is for using: to give flavor, to offer it; otherwise, "it becomes insipid and doesn't work."

But salt has another feature when "it's used properly," said

Pope Francis: "you don't taste the salt." So "the taste of salt" doesn't alter the taste of other things; so that "we taste the flavor of every food," which becomes better and more tasty. And that's Christian originality: when we proclaim the faith, with this salt," anyone who receives it, "receives it in their own way, just as they have their own kinds of food."

"Christian originality," said the bishop of Rome, "isn't uniformity. It takes each person as they are, with their personality, their character, their culture," and leaves them as it found them, "because this is richness; it gives them something more, gives them flavor." But if there was a tendency to uniformity, "it would be as if all were seasoned in the same way." The same would happen if we behaved "as when the cook puts in too much salt": we would only taste the salt and "not the flavor of that food seasoned with salt."

Christian originality lies in this: everyone remains who they are, with the gifts the Lord has given them. "Each of us is different from everyone else"; so Christian salt is that which "brings out the quality of each person. That's the salt we must give" and not just store it. Or at least not just store it till it loses its strength.

And "for salt not to lose its strength," there are two things to do "which should go together." The pope explained them like this: "First of all, use it, for food, for the service of others, for the service of people. We are talking about the salt of faith, hope, and love: give it, give it, give!" The other thing is to go out, "toward the maker of salt, the creator, the one who makes the salt. Salt can't be kept only to give out in preaching. It also needs to go outward, in prayer, worship. And thus salt is kept without losing its taste. By worshiping the Lord, I go out of myself to the Lord; and by proclaiming the gospel I go out of myself to give the message."

If we don't go this way "to give salt," the pope concluded, "it will stay in its jar, and we will become museum Christians" who can only display salt in its jar. But this will be a "salt without taste, a salt that doesn't do anything."

THE WISDOM OF CHRISTIANS

Friday, May 24, 2013
SIR 6:5–17; MK 10:1–12

"In the prayer in the Latin missal for this morning's Mass, dedicated to Mary Help of Christians, we ask for two graces," said Pope Francis in his homily today, May 24, during the Mass in the chapel of St. Martha's Guest House. "The two graces are: to endure with patience and to overcome by love the things that oppress us from within and outside." These are particularly Christian graces. But "enduring with patience isn't easy," the pope admitted. In fact, "when difficulties come from outside and we also have heart and soul problems, problems inside us, it isn't easy to endure them with patience. It's easier to become impatient."

So what does "enduring" mean? Enduring means "bearing a difficulty. But does it mean carrying a difficulty on our back? No," explained the Holy Father, "enduring means taking on the difficulty and bearing it, with fortitude, so that the difficulty doesn't get us down. That's a Christian virtue. St. Paul often speaks about it. So enduring means not letting the difficulty get the better of us. A Christian has the strength not to let go, but to carry the load, to carry on." This isn't an easy task because we become discouraged and we feel the urge to "let go and say: All right, let's do what we can and no more! Enduring is a grace and we should ask for it when we are in difficulties."

The other grace about which the pope spoke was that of overcoming by love. "We can overcome in so many ways," he said, "but the grace we are asking for today is the grace of victory through love. It isn't easy." Love is "that gentleness which Jesus taught us. That's the victory." The apostle John, said the pope, "tells us in his first letter: this is our victory, our faith. Our faith is this: to believe in Jesus who has taught us love and taught us to love everybody. And the proof that we love is when we pray for our enemies."

The Holy Father gave as an example the wisdom of old people: "When old people have lived this way, it's beautiful to look at them. They have a beautiful look, a serene happiness. They don't speak much but their hearts are patient and full of love. They know how to forgive their enemies, they know how to pray for their enemies. There are so many Christians like that." But if "we go the other way," that of not forgiving, denying love, then "we are impatient and we grow tired." "Victory," he concluded, "is faith in Jesus who taught us the way of love, and defeat is going the other way. We find so many sad, discouraged Christians because they have lacked this grace of enduring with patience and overcoming with love!"

Speaking at the beginning of the Mass about the feast for the day, Pope Francis recalled Mary Help of Christians and said that today "the whole church prays for China, for Chinese Christians. This morning we offer Mass for that great and noble people, the Chinese, for Chinese Christians, for the Madonna to help and guard them."

CHRISTIAN WELCOME

Saturday, May 25, 2013
SIR 17:1–15; MK 10:13–16

Christians who ask to come in should never find the doors closed. Churches are not offices where you present documents and letters when seeking to enter God's grace. "We mustn't institute an eighth sacrament of pastoral border control!" Christian welcome was the subject of Pope Francis' reflection in his homily at the Mass he concelebrated with Cardinal Agostino Cacciavillan, among others, this morning, Saturday, May 25, in the chapel of St. Martha's Guest House. Commenting on Mark's gospel (10:13-16), the pope recalled Jesus' rebuke to his disciples when they wanted to keep the children away from him, who had been brought by people wanting him to touch them. The disciples suggested "a general blessing and then everybody out," but what does the gospel say? That Jesus was indignant, replied the pope, saying, "Let the little children come to me; do not stop them, for it is to such as these that the kingdom of heaven belongs."

The faith of the people of God is a simple faith. For example, perhaps they don't know how to explain correctly who the Virgin is but for that, said the Holy Father, "you need to go to a theologian: he will explain very well to you who Mary is." But he immediately added, "if you want to know how to love Mary, go to the people of God, who will teach you that well, better." This is a people "who always come to ask Jesus for something" and sometimes rather insistently. As he went on to tell: "I remember once, during the feast day of the patron saint in the city of Salta, a poor woman was asking a priest for a blessing. The priest said: But madam, you were at Mass! And then he went on to explain the whole theology of blessing during Mass. Oh, thank you, Father, said the woman. But when the priest had gone, she turned to a different priest and asked him: Give me a blessing. She had not taken in all that long explanation because she had a different need, the need to be touched by the Lord. That's the faith we are seeking and we must always find because it's aroused by the Spirit. We must enable it, let it grow, help it to grow."

So the pope went on to explain Jesus' attitude when he rebuked the apostles, who were preventing people from coming up to him. The apostles were not doing this to be unkind; they simply wanted to help Jesus. The people of Jericho had done the same when they tried to silence the blind man, who was yelling to attract Jesus' attention and be cured. The pope explained, it was as if they had said: "Protocol doesn't allow this: this is the second person of the Trinity; what do you think you're doing? That reminds me of so many Christians…"

In order to explain things better, the pope gave a few examples. In particular, when an engaged couple wanting to get married comes to the parish office, and instead of support or congratulations all they are given is a list of the costs of the ceremony or they are asked if their documents are all in order. So sometimes, said the pope, "they find the door shut." Here someone who has the chance "to open the door, thanking God for this new marriage," doesn't do so and the door is closed. So often "we are controllers of the faith instead of becoming enablers of people's faith." "And that's something," the pope added, which "began in Jesus' time with the apostles."

What is happening is "a temptation that we have to take over the Lord." The pope gave another example: a young single mother went to church in her parish and asked for her child to be baptized and got the reply from a "Christian": "No, you can't, you aren't married." And the pope continued: "Look at this girl who has had the courage to take her pregnancy to term" and not have an abortion: "What does she find? A closed door. And this happens to so many women. That isn't good pastoral care. It distances people from the Lord, rather than opening doors. And so when we go that way, behave like that, we don't treat people well, the people of God. Jesus instituted seven sacraments, but by this attitude we institute an eighth, the sacrament of pastoral border control."

"Jesus becomes indignant when he sees such things, because

who suffers? The faithful people, the people he loves so much." Jesus, the pope explained concluding his homily, wants everyone to come close to him. "Let us think of God's holy people, simple people, who want to come close to Jesus. And let us think of all the Christians of goodwill who make mistakes and instead of opening the door to them, we close it. And let us ask the Lord that all those who approach the church may find an open door, so that they can experience the love of Jesus."

GOD'S TIME

Monday, May 27, 2013
SIR 17:19–27; MK 10:17–27

The lure of the temporary, the feeling of being masters of our own time, and the culture of comfort at all costs often prevent people from following Jesus closely. "We think these things are wealth," but really they don't make us "go forward," said Pope Francis, commenting on the gospel story in Mark (10:17-27), read this Monday morning, May 27, during the Mass celebrated in the chapel of St. Martha's Guest House.

The evangelist tells us about a rich man who approaches Jesus to ask him how he can get eternal life. "This man," the pope explained, "was a good man. He goes to find Jesus and kneels before him. He was a man with a devout heart, a religious man, a just man. He goes to Jesus because he feels something within himself. He feels he wants to go further, to follow Jesus more closely. It was the Holy Spirit impelling him."

He assures Jesus that he keeps the commandments. And asks him how he can go forward. But when Jesus, "who loves him," asks him to sell all his goods before coming back to follow him, "this good man, this just man—a man impelled by the Holy Spirit to go further, closer to Jesus—becomes discouraged. At Jesus' words his face clouded, and he went sadly away. And Jesus looked around and said to his disciples: How hard it is for those who have wealth to enter the kingdom of God," the Holy Father recalled.

So, he explained, "wealth is a hindrance, something that doesn't make the road toward the kingdom of God easy. Each of us has our wealth, but often these riches prevent us from getting close to Jesus" and sometimes they also bring us "sadness."

"All of us," urged the pope, "must examine our consciences about what riches we have that prevent us from getting close to Jesus on the road of life." It's wealth that comes from our culture. Our primary wealth "is comfort. The comfort culture makes us not very brave, makes us lazy, also makes us selfish." Sometimes "comfort anesthetizes us," because at the end of the day "we enjoy our comfort." So when we are deciding whether to have a child, we are often ruled by comfort or well-being. The pope imagined a conversation between a married couple: "No, not more than one child, no! Because we won't be able to go on holiday, we won't be able to go about, we won't be able to buy the house: no! It's all very well following the Lord, but only up to a point…" And the pope commented: "That's what comfort does to us. We all know how comfort affects us. But it casts us down, it robs us of our courage, that strong courage to walk close to Jesus." For "that's the primary wealth of our culture today. The culture of comfort."

Besides this, the pope pointed out another thing that "prevents us from being close to Jesus: the lure of the temporary. We are in love with the temporary," whereas Jesus' proposals are definitive. We like the temporary "because we are afraid of God's time," which is definitive time.

And as often happens, the pope offered a memory from his personal experience: "I heard about someone who wanted to be a priest, but for ten years, no longer." And the same thing happens with every couple who get married thinking: "as long as love lasts and then we'll see." This is "the lure of the temporary," the second sort of "wealth" that delights people today. In particular, it drives them to "become masters of their own time: let's take things a little at a time."

Comfort and keeping things temporary are the two sorts of wealth in our society that "prevent us from going forward." On the other hand, the pope's thoughts went out to "so many men and women who have left their country to go out as missionaries, for the whole of their lives"; and to "so many men and women who have left home to get married and remained till the end of their lives." That, he said, "is following Jesus closely, it's definitive." Whereas "something temporary is not following Jesus; the temporary is our own ground," where "we are masers."

So the pope urged us: "In the face of Jesus' invitation, in the face of our two sorts of cultural wealth, let us think about the disciples," who "were disconcerted. We too can be disconcerted by these words of Jesus. And when Jesus explained, they were even more astounded." So, the pope's final invitation was "let us ask the Lord to give us the courage to go forward, ridding ourselves of this culture of well-being by hope," which is "the end of the road where he is waiting for us, in time; not with the little momentary hope, which doesn't work any longer."

THE CHRISTIAN'S REWARD

Tuesday, May 28, 2013
SIR 35:1–12; MK 10:28–31

Suffering is part of life. But for the Christian, called to follow the same way as Christ, it becomes an added value. Especially when it takes the form of persecution, because of the spirit of the world which doesn't tolerate Christian witness. That, in brief, was the pope's reflection during the Mass celebrated in the chapel of St. Martha's Guest House on Tuesday morning, May 28. Commenting on the gospel of the day (Mark 10:28-31), the pope returned to Jesus' conversation with the rich young man who asked him how he could get eternal life. The pope recalled that Peter had heard Jesus' warnings about wealth, which makes it "so difficult to enter the kingdom of God."

After the Lord's words, Peter asks him, "Look, we have left everything and followed you. What will our wages be? What will be our reward?" Perhaps Jesus' answer "is a bit ironical: but yes, you and all of you who have left house, brothers, sisters, mother, children or fields will receive a hundredfold." But he warns them that they will have to face "persecutions," described as the wages, or rather, "the reward of the disciple."

Jesus promises those who follow him that they will belong "to the family of Christians" and reminds them that "we are all brothers." But he also warns that "there will be persecutions, difficulties." Returning to the same subject he says, "Anyone who follows me, must take the same road that I have taken." A road, the pope explains, that leads us to humble ourselves and which "ends on the cross. We will always meet difficulties that come from the world and also persecutions, because he himself walked that way first. When a Christian has no difficulty in life and everything goes well, everything is fine, then something isn't right." We need to consider whether we haven't given in to the temptation to follow the spirit of the world rather than Jesus.

Following the Lord, repeated the bishop of Rome, means doing so completely. Following Jesus can't be merely a cultural expression. Even less can it be a way to gain more power. With regard to this, the pope observed that "the history of the church is full of that, beginning with certain emperors; then so many rulers, so many

people. And even some—I don't want to say many but some—
priests, even bishops. There are not that many but some think that
following Jesus is pursuing a career." That idea, said Pope Francis,
can be found in biographies of saints from a long time ago. Then it
was usual to read that "from childhood he had wanted to pursue a
church career. That's the way they put it, it was a way of speaking.
But so many Christians, tempted by the spirit of the world," added the pope, "think that following Jesus" is a good thing because
"that's the way to pursue a career, to get ahead." However, "that's
not the right spirit"; rather, it's Peter's attitude when he asks: "And
what about us, what career can we make?" But Jesus' answer was:
"Yes, I'll give you everything, with persecution."

It isn't possible, said the bishop of Rome, "to take away the
cross from the way of Jesus. It's always there." Of course, the
Christian mustn't make trouble for himself. "It's not that." He
added: "The Christian follows Jesus out of love, and when you
follow Jesus out of love, the devil's envy does so many things.
The spirit of the world won't tolerate it, won't tolerate Christian
witness. Think of Mother Teresa," as a positive figure who "has
done so many fine things for others. The spirit of the world never
says that every day blessed Teresa spent hours in worship. Never.
It reduces Christian activity to doing social good. As if Christian
life were a varnish, a patina of Christianity. But the proclamation
of Jesus is not a patina." It penetrates the bones, it goes straight
"to the heart." It gets inside us and changes us. And that's what
the spirit of the world won't tolerate; it won't tolerate it and so
persecutions come.

Hence the invitation to think of Jesus' answer: There is no one
who has left house or brothers or sisters or mother or father or
children or fields "for my sake and for the sake of the gospel, who
will not receive a hundredfold now, in this age, houses, brothers
and sisters, but with persecutions. Let's not forget it." To follow
Jesus with love, step by step: That is following Christ, the Holy

Father concluded. But the spirit of the world will continue not to tolerate it and will make Christians suffer. But it's a suffering like that of Jesus: "Let us ask for this grace: to follow Jesus along the road that he showed us, he taught us. That's the beautiful way: he never leaves us alone, never. He is always with us."

THE TRIUMPHALISM OF CHRISTIANS

Wednesday, May 29, 2013
SIR 36:5–6, 10–17; MK 10:32–45

The triumph belonging to Christians is that which comes by way of human weakness, the weakness of the cross. Allowing ourselves to be tempted by other triumphs, worldly triumphs, means giving way to the temptation to conceive of a "Christianity without the cross," a "halfway Christianity." Humility was the center of Pope Francis' reflection during the Mass celebrated this morning, Wednesday, May 29, in the chapel of St. Martha's Guest House.

Today's gospel (Mark 10:32-45) describes Jesus' journey toward Jerusalem, followed by his disciples. "They were on the road that went up to Jerusalem," the pope explained, "and Jesus went ahead. Determined. We may also imagine in haste." Thinking about what the disciples were feeling at that moment—they were "alarmed" and "dismayed"—the Holy Father wanted to point out Jesus' behavior as he revealed the truth to them: "'See, we are going up to Jerusalem, and the Son of Man will be delivered to the chief priests and scribes; they will condemn him to death and they will kill him, but after three days he will rise again.'"

The disciples thought it would be better to stop. And at the same time, the pope noted, they began to discuss "how to organize the church." So James and John "went to Jesus to ask him for the posts of head of government." But the others were also "discussing and wondering who among them would be the most important" in that church they wanted to organize. Christ, said the pope, was going ahead to fulfill his mission, while his disciples had stopped to discuss "another project, another way of looking at the church."

Thus they underwent the same temptation Jesus had suffered in the wilderness, when "the devil proposed a different way to him," and challenged him to work "a miracle, something everyone was asking for." Like throwing himself down from the temple and saving himself, so that everyone could see the miracle and be redeemed.

Jesus was offered the same temptation by Peter. When Jesus spoke about the cross, the bishop of Rome recalled, the apostle, who had just recognized him to be the Son of God, begged him to give up the idea. "And Jesus says to him: Satan! And rejects the temptation."

Today, the pope stressed, the danger is to succumb to the "temptation of a Christianity without the cross. A halfway Christianity. That's a temptation." But there is also another temptation, added the pope, "that of a Christianity with the cross but without Jesus," about which, he said, perhaps he might speak on another occasion. Returning to the subject of the homily, the pope explained that it was about the question of triumph. "We want triumph now," he said, "without the cross. A worldly triumph, a reasonable triumph." By way of example, he quoted the gospel story of Christ's own temptation: "Worship me and I will give you everything." "That," noted the pope, "was as long as he didn't do what the Father wanted him to do."

"Triumphalism in the church," the pope continued, "stops the church. The triumphalism of us Christians stops Christians. A triumphalist church is a halfway church." A church that was content to be "well organized, with all its offices, everything in order, everything fine, efficient," but which denied its martyrs, would be "a church that only thinks of triumphs, success, which doesn't keep the rule of Jesus: the rule of triumph through failure. Human failure, the failure of the cross. And that's a temptation we all have."

The pope recalled an example from his own life: "Once I was in a dark place in my spiritual life, and I asked a grace from the Lord. I went to preach the Exercises to some nuns and on the final day they made their confessions. An old nun came to confess. She was over eighty but her eyes were bright, even luminous. She was a woman of God. Then I saw how much she was a woman of God so I said to her: 'Sister, as a penance, pray for me, because I need a grace, won't you? If you ask the Lord for me, he will surely give it to me.' She stopped a moment, as if she were praying and said this to me: 'Of course the Lord will give you the grace, but make no mistake: he'll do so in his own divine way.' That did me so much good: to hear that the Lord always gives us what we ask for, but does so in his own divine way." That way, explained the pope, "involves the cross. Not through masochism, no, no: for love, love till the end."

Concluding the homily, the Holy Father invited everyone to ask the Lord "for the grace not to be a halfway church, a triumphalist church, with great successes." "If the church is humble," he said, "it walks with decision like Jesus; it goes onward, onward, onward."

ETERNITY WON'T BE BORING

Feast of the Visitation

Friday, May 31, 2013
ZEP 3:14–18; LK 1:39–56

So many Christians don't experience joy. And even when they are in church to praise God, it feels more like a funeral to them than a joyful celebration. But if they learned to go out of themselves and thank God, "they'd really understand that joy which set us free."

Christian joy was the focus of Pope Francis' homily this morning, Friday, May 31, during the Mass he concelebrated in the chapel of St. Martha's Guest House.

"Today's two readings," the pope began, referring to the passages taken from the book of the prophet Zephaniah (3:14-18) and Luke's gospel (1:39-56), "tell us about joy, happiness: 'Sing aloud, shout!' says Zephaniah. Rejoice and exult with all your heart! 'The Lord is in your midst'; don't be afraid; 'Don't let your hands grow weak!' the Lord is strong; he will rejoice over you. And he will also rejoice over us. He is joyful too. 'He will exult over you with loud singing.' Listen to what beautiful things are said about joy!"

In the gospel story joy is the hallmark of Mary's visit to Elizabeth. "The Madonna goes to visit Elizabeth," recalled the Holy Father. And presenting the image of Mary as a mother who is always in a hurry, which he had done the previous Sunday in the Roman parish of Sts. Elizabeth and Zechariah, Pope Francis dwelled on that "baby leaping in Elizabeth's womb," as Elizabeth herself told Mary: "For as soon as I heard the sound of your greeting, the child in my womb leapt for joy."

"It's all joy. But we Christians, noted the bishop of Rome, aren't used to talking about joy, or happiness. I think we often prefer grumbling! What is joy? The key to understanding this joy is what the gospel says: 'Elizabeth was filled with the Holy Spirit.' The one who gives us joy is the Holy Spirit. Even in the first prayer of this Mass we asked for the grace of docility to the Holy Spirit, the one who gives us joy."

Then the pope spoke about another aspect of the joy that comes from the Spirit. "Let's think," he said, "about that moment when the Madonna and St. Joseph take Jesus to the temple to fulfill the law. The gospel says they went to do what was written in the law." There are also two old people in the temple; but, he noted, the gospel doesn't tell us that they went there to fulfill the law, but rather that they were impelled "by the Holy Spirit. The Spirit brings them to the temple." So when they see Jesus, both "say a prayer of praise: this is the Messiah, blessed be the Lord!" Their faithfulness over so many years of waiting for the Holy Spirit to come and bring them joy also creates a spontaneous liturgy of joy.

Pope Francis confided, "I like to think: the young people fulfill the law; the old people have the freedom to let the Spirit guide them. And that's wonderful! It's the Spirit who guides us. He is the author of joy, the creator of joy. And this joy in the Spirit gives us true Christian freedom. Without joy we Christians can't become free. We become slaves to our sadness."

Then the pope quoted "the great Paul VI," recalling that he said "we can't carry forward the gospel with sad, disheartened, discouraged Christians; it's not possible. That attitude is a bit funereal." Rather, Christian joy comes from praising God.

"But what does it mean to praise God?" asked the pope. "To praise him freely, as the grace that he gives us is free" was his reply. Then turning to someone who was present at the celebration, he said: "I can ask you who are here at Mass: do you praise God? Or do you just ask God and thank God? But do you praise God?" That, he repeated, means "going out of ourselves to praise God, to spend our time praising."

At this point the pope referred to one of the criticisms that is often directed at priests: "This Mass you are saying is so long." Turning to those present, he explained, "if you don't praise God and don't choose freely to spend time praising God, then of course the Mass is long! But if you come with this attitude of joy, of praising God, it's beautiful." What's more, "eternity will be that: praising God. But it won't be boring, it will be wonderful. That joy sets us free."

"And I want to add," he said in conclusion, "one last thing: it's she, the Madonna, who brings joy. The church calls her cause of our joy, *causa nostrae laetitiae*. Why? Because she brings our greatest joy, she brings Jesus. And when she brings Jesus it makes 'that child leap in his mother's womb.' She brings Jesus. By her prayer she makes the Holy Spirit break out. He breaks out on that day of Pentecost; he was there. We should pray to the Madonna that by bringing Jesus she may give us the grace of joy, of freedom; give us the grace to praise, to freely offer a prayer of praise, because he is worthy of praise, always."

THE SCANDAL OF THE INCARNATION
Feast of Justin Martyr
Saturday, June 1, 2013
SIR 51:12–20; MK 11:27–33

The "scandal" of a God who became human and died on the cross was the subject of Pope Francis' homily this morning, Saturday, June 1, during the Mass he concelebrated in the chapel of St. Martha's Guest House.

The memory of Justin Martyr, whose feast day it was, gave the pope the opportunity to reflect on what lies consistently at the center of every Christian's faith: the cross. "We can do all the social work we want," he said, "and they will say: how good the church is, what good social work the church does. But if we say we do it because these people are Christ's flesh, they are scandalized."

Without the incarnation of the Word the foundation of our faith is lacking, as the pope stressed: "This is the truth, this is Jesus' revelation. This presence of Jesus incarnate. That's the point." If it's forgotten, Christ's disciples will always be strongly "tempted to do good works without the scandal of the incarnate Word, without the scandal of the cross."

Justin was witness to this truth; it was through the scandal of the cross that he attracted persecution from the world. He proclaimed the God who came among us and identified with his creatures. The proclamation of Christ crucified and risen dismays his hearers, but he continues to bear witness to this truth through the consistency of his life. "The church," said the pope, "isn't a cultural, religious, or social organization; it isn't that. The church is Jesus' family. The church confesses that Jesus is the Son of God, come in the flesh. That's the scandal and that's why they persecuted Jesus."

The pope referred to the gospel passage from Mark (11:27-33), read during the liturgy, and in particular to the question put to Jesus by the priests, scribes, and elders of Jerusalem: "By what authority do you do this?" Jesus in his turn answers with a question: "Was the baptism of John from heaven or from men?" and thus doesn't go along with their false curiosity. Only later in front of the high priest, who was "the people's authority," does he answer what the scribes and elders had asked him. He did not answer them because he knew that their real objective was "to set a trap for him." They try in various ways, as the pope recalled: "But tell me, teacher, should people pay taxes to Caesar?" Or: "Tell me, teacher, this woman was taken in adultery. Should we fulfill the law of Moses or is there another way?" Every question is a trap to corner him, to make him say something wrong, and to find a pretext to condemn him.

But why was Jesus a problem? "It wasn't because he worked miracles," replied the pope. "And neither was it because he preached and spoke about the people's freedom." "The problem that scandalized these people," he said, "was what the demons screamed at Jesus: 'You are the Son of God, you are the Holy One.' That, that is the point." What is scandalous about Jesus is his nature as God incarnate. And just as they did to him, they set traps for us in our lives; what scandalizes people about the church is the mystery of the incarnation of the Word: which can't be taken away, which the demons can't take away." Even now we often hear it said: "But you Christians should be a bit more normal, like other people, reasonable; don't be so rigid." Behind this invitation there is really the request not to proclaim that "God became man" because "the incarnation of the Word is the scandal."

When the high priest asks him: "Are you the Christ, the Son of God?" Jesus answers yes and is immediately condemned to death. "This lies at the center of his persecution," stressed the pope. In fact, "if we become reasonable Christians, social Christians, who only do good works, what will the consequences be? That we will never have martyrs." On the other hand, when we say that "the Son of God came and became flesh, when we preach the scandal of the cross, persecutions will come, the cross will come."

In conclusion, Pope Francis urged the faithful to ask the Lord that "they not be ashamed to live with this scandal of the cross." And he invited them to ask God for the wisdom "not to let ourselves be trapped by the spirit of the world, which always makes good-mannered, civilized suggestions, good suggestions." Behind these requests, he warned, people are denying "the fact that the Word has become incarnate, a fact that "scandalizes" and "destroys the work of the devil."

THE GREAT FORGETTERS

Feast of the Martyrs of Uganda

Monday, June 3, 2013
Tob 1:1–2; 2:1–9; Mk 12:1–12

This morning, Monday, June 3, Pope Francis' thoughts turned to his predecessor, John XXIII—"a model of holiness," he said. He was recalling the fiftieth anniversary of his death, but he wanted above all to reassert his testimony at a time when, even in the church, there are those who choose the path of corruption instead of the way of love as a response to God's gift to humanity. The pope also alluded to the witness of holiness in the initial prayer of the Mass at St. Martha's Guest House, when he recalled the anniversary of Sts. Carlo Lwanga and his companions, the Uganda martyrs.

During his homily Pope Francis wanted to share with those present some reflections on the gospel of Mark (2:1-12). He began: "I have been thinking about three sorts of Christians in the church: the sinners, the corrupt, the saints. We don't need to say much about the sinners, because they are all of us. We know ourselves from the inside and we know what a sinner is. And if any of us doesn't feel like that, they should pay a visit to the spiritual doctor: something is wrong." The Christians the Holy Father dwelled on longer were the corrupt. In the gospel parable, he explained, Jesus speaks of the great love of the owner of a vineyard, a symbol of the people of God: "He has called us with love, he looks after us. But then he gives us freedom, he gives us all this love 'on lease.' It's as if he said to us: Keep and watch over my love as I watch over you. And the conversation between God and us is: Look after love. Everything begins with this love."

But then the tenants, to whom the vineyard is rented out, "feel they are strong, they feel they are independent of God," explained the Holy Father. And thus "they took over that vineyard; and they lost their connection with the owner of the vineyard: We are the owners! And when someone comes to collect from them the share of the harvest that belongs to the owner, they beat him, they insult him, they threaten him." That means losing touch with God, no longer needing "that owner." That's what "the corrupt do, those who are sinners like all of us, but have gone one step further": they have "become confirmed in their sin and no longer feel any need of God." Or at least they delude themselves that they don't feel it because, explained the bishop of Rome, "we have this connection with God in our genetic code. And as they can't deny that, they make a special God: themselves."

These are the corrupt. And "this is also a danger for us: becoming corrupt. They exist in Christian communities and they do so much harm. Jesus talks to the doctors of the law, the Pharisees, who were corrupt. And he tells them that they are whited sepulchers. And in Christian communities the corrupt are like that. People say oh, he's a good Christian, he belongs to that confraternity; he's good, good, he's one of us. But it's not so: they are out for themselves. Judas began as an avaricious sinner; he finished in corruption. It's a dangerous road, the road of independence. The corrupt are great forgetters; they have forgotten the love with which the Lord created the vineyard, created them. They've cut off their connection with this love. And they have become self-worshipers. What a lot of harm is done by the corrupt in Christian communities! May the Lord deliver us from slipping into the road of corruption!"

But in the church there are also saints. "And now," said the pope, "I'm glad to be talking about saints, and I'm pleased to be doing so on the fiftieth anniversary of the death of Pope John, a model of holiness." In the gospel parable, explained Pope Francis, "the saints are those who go to get the rent and know what is awaiting them. But they have to do it and they do their duty. The saints, those who obey the Lord, those who worship the Lord, those who have not lost the memory of the love with which the Lord created the vineyard. Saints in the church. And just as the corrupt do so much harm in the church, the saints do so much good."

And he concluded: "The apostle John says of the corrupt that they are the Anti-Christ, they are in our midst, but they don't belong to us. From the saints God's word speaks to us like light: they are those who will worship before God's throne. Let us ask the Lord today for the grace to feel that we are sinners. The grace not to become corrupt: sinners yes, corrupt no. And the grace to walk along the way of holiness."

Let's Learn the Language of Children

Tuesday, June 4, 2013
Tob 2:9–14; Mk 12:13–17

Pope Francis spoke again about corruption. This morning, Tuesday, June 4, he offered a reflection on the language usually spoken by the corrupt, which is the language of hypocrisy: the same, he said, as that used by Satan in the wilderness when he tempted Jesus. The pope spoke about this during the Mass in the chapel of St. Martha's Guest House.

During the homily the pope took his cue from the gospel passage from Mark (12:13-17), in which the evangelist tells how "some Pharisees and Herodians" tried to trap Jesus. "Only some," the pope specified, "because they weren't all bad." These "went to Jesus in order to catch him out. They pretended to know the truth, but they had other intentions, to make him fall into a trap. They came to him and said: 'Teacher, we know that you are sincere, and show deference to no one, for you do not regard people with partiality, but teach the way of God in accordance with the truth.' But they didn't believe what they were saying. It was flattery." This is "the flatterer's language, which uses soft, sweet words that are too sugary."

Yesterday, the Holy Father recalled, "we spoke about the corrupt. Today we find the language of the corrupt. So what is their language? It's the language of hypocrisy. It's not we who say this, not I who am saying this, but Jesus, who knows their hypocrisy."

Hypocrisy he stressed again is "the language of the corrupt. They don't love the truth. They only love themselves and so they seek to deceive and involve others in their lies, their deceit. They have lying hearts; they can't tell the truth. This is the same language that Satan used in the wilderness: you're hungry: you can change this stone into bread; and then: why do you work so hard; throw yourself down from the temple. That language, which seems so persuasive, leads to error, leads to lies."

The pope continued, returning to the gospel story, "Those Pharisees who are so friendly in their language, are the same ones who will go on the Thursday night to arrest him in the Garden of Olives and on Friday will bring him before Pilate. And they will use the same talk with Pilate: we have no king but Caesar." That language is an attempt at diabolical persuasion. In fact, those who at that moment "praised" Christ end up betraying him and sending him to the cross. Looking them in the face Jesus calls them hypocrites!"

So hypocrisy is the language of corruption and certainly not "the language of truth, because truth," said the bishop of Rome, "is never on its own; it always comes with love. There is no truth without love. Love is the first truth. And if there is no love, there is no truth." Hypocrites, on the other hand, "want a truth enslaved to their own interests." Even in them there is a kind of love but it's "self-love," a sort of "narcissistic idolatry that leads them to betray others and to abuses of trust." Instead, "the mildness Jesus wants from us has nothing, nothing to do with that flattery, that sugary way of going on. Nothing. Mildness is simple, like that of a child. And a child is not a hypocrite, because he isn't corrupt. When Jesus tells us: let your speech be: yes, yes, no, no, with the mind of a child, he is telling us the opposite of what the corrupt say."

All of us, Pope Francis recognized, actually have "a certain inner weakness" and we like "people to say nice things about us."

We all like it because at the end of the day we all have that little bit of vanity. The corrupt know this and by their language "they try to weaken us." So "let's think carefully today," he recommended, "about the language we use ourselves: do we speak truthfully, with love, or do we use a bit of that other language," which leads us to say nice things we don't really mean? "Let our speaking be that of the gospel," the Holy Father prayed. And "let us ask the Lord that we may always speak like the simple, like children, like children of God: that is, speak truthfully with love."

LIFE AT THE BOTTOM

Wednesday, June 5, 2013
TOB 3:1–11, 16; MK 12:18–27

Pope Francis prayed for people who live "at the bottom," in conditions "on the edge," who have lost hope, during the Mass this morning, Wednesday, June 5, in the chapel of St. Martha's Guest House.

It was the readings for the day that suggested thinking about so many who feel abandoned and suffer in their lives. In the first reading, taken from the book of Tobit (3:1-11, 16-17), the pope focused on the experiences of Tobit and Sarah, the story of two people suffering on the verge of despair between life and death. Both are searching for "a way out," which they find by complaining. "They don't blaspheme but they complain," said the pope.

"Complaining to God isn't a sin," he said. And he immediately went on to mention: "A priest I know once told a woman who was complaining to God about the disasters in her life: But go ahead, it's a form of prayer. The Lord listens, he hears our complaints." Then the pope recalled the examples of Job and Jeremiah, who, he noted, "complained even with curses: not against the Lord but the situation. What's more," he added, complaining "is human," because "there are so many people who are suffering in their lives." He referred to the photo of the starving child published yesterday afternoon on the first page of L'Osservatore Romano. "How many are there like that?" he asked. "What about Syria, refugees, all those people?" And "think of hospitals: what about all those suffering terminal illnesses?"

Pope Francis answered by referring to the third person mentioned in the readings of the day, the woman described in the gospel passage (Mark 12:18-27). Addressing Jesus, the Sadducees presented her as in "a laboratory, aseptically, as a moral case." But "when we speak about these people who are in situations on the edge," we should do so "with our hearts close to theirs"; we should think "of these people who are suffering so much with our hearts, with our gut-feelings." And we shouldn't be happy "when these situations are spoken about in an academic, instead of a human, way," treating people as statistics. "In the church there are so many people in this situation." And if anyone asks what to do, the pope's reply was "Do what Jesus says: pray, pray for them." Suffering people, he explained, "should get to my heart, I should worry about them. My brother is suffering, my sister is suffering; this is the mystery of the communion of saints. Pray: Lord, look at this person, weeping, suffering. Pray, if I can put it like that, with our own flesh." Pray with our flesh, "not with ideas; pray from the heart," he repeated.

Lastly, the pope pointed out how in the first reading there is a little phrase that opens the door to hope, which can help us in prayer. It's the expression "at that very moment." When Tobit was praying, "at that very moment Sarah" was praying; and "at that very moment" the prayers of both of them were heard in the glorious presence of God. "Prayer," said the pope, "always reaches the glorious presence of God. Always when it's prayer from the heart." On the other hand, when we look at someone suffering merely as "a moral case," it "never reaches that presence, because it never goes out from us, it doesn't concern us, it's an intellectual game."

Hence the invitation to think of those suffering. It's a condition which Jesus knows well, to the limit of abandonment on the cross. "Let us speak to Jesus today in this Mass," concluded Pope Francis, "about all these brothers and sisters who are suffering so much, who are in that situation. So that our prayer reaches him and may give a little hope to all of us."

Unmasking Hidden Idols

Thursday, June 6, 2013
Tob 6:11; 7:1, 9–14; 8:4–7; Mk 12:28–34

Pope Francis invited us to discover "the idols hidden in so many sore places we have in our personalities" and to "hunt out the idol of worldliness, which leads us to become God's enemies," during Mass this morning, Thursday, June 6, in the chapel of St. Martha's Guest House.

He went on to urge us to "take the way of love for God," to undertake "a journey to reach" his kingdom. His reflection focused on the gospel passage from Mark (12:28-34), in which Jesus answers the scribe who asks him which is the most important of all the commandments. First, the pope noted that Jesus doesn't reply with an explanation but by quoting God's word: "Hear, O Israel! The Lord our God, the Lord is one." Those, he said, "are not the words of Jesus." In fact Jesus replies to the scribe, as he did to Satan during the temptations, "with the word of God, not with his own words." And he does so by quoting "Israel's creed, that which is said by Jews every day and several times a day: Shema Israel! Remember, Israel, to love God alone."

The pope suggested that perhaps the scribe "wasn't a saint, and was trying to test Jesus and also to trap him." In short, he didn't have the best intentions, because "when Jesus replies with the word of God," it means it was a test. "And we see this also when the scribe says to him: 'You are right, Teacher,' giving the impression that he is approving the reply. That's why Jesus says to him, 'You are not far from the kingdom of God. You know the theory well, you know very well that this is so but you are not far. You still have one thing lacking to get to the kingdom of God.'" That means that you have to undertake "a journey to reach the kingdom of God"; you have to "put this commandment into practice."

So "professing God must be done by the way we live, on our life's journey. It isn't enough," the pope warned, "to say I believe in God, the one God." We must ask ourselves how to live by this commandment. In fact, we go on "living as if he were not the only God," and as if "there were other divinities at our disposal." That's what Pope Francis called "the danger of idolatry," which is "brought to us by the spirit of the world." And Jesus was always clear about this: "No to the spirit of the world." So at the Last Supper "he asks the Father to defend us from the spirit of the world, because it leads us to idolatry." And in the fourth chapter of his letter, the apostle James says very clearly that anyone who is a friend of the world is an enemy of God. There is no other option. Jesus himself uses similar words, the Holy Father recalled: "Either God or money: you can't serve money and God."

For Pope Francis it is the spirit of the world that leads us to idolatry and it does so cunningly. "I'm sure," he said, "that none of you goes up to a tree to worship it as an idol"; that "none of us have statues to worship at home." But, he warned, "idolatry is subtle; we have our hidden idols, and the way to reach the kingdom of God is a way that includes unmasking these hidden idols." It's a demanding task, since often we keep them "well hidden," as Rachel did when she fled with her husband Jacob from the house of Laban her father. She had taken the idols and hidden them under the camel saddle that she was sitting on. So when her father asked her to get up, she replied "with excuses, with arguments," in order to keep the idols hidden. According to the pope, we do the same, we too keep our own idols "hidden away." That means "we must search for them and destroy them, as Moses destroyed the golden calf in the wilderness."

But how can we unmask these idols? The Holy Father offered a criterion. Idols are those things that make us do the opposite of the commandment: "Hear, O Israel! The Lord our God, the Lord is one." So "the way to love God—thou shalt love the Lord thy God with all thy heart, with all thy soul—is the way of love. It's a way of faithfulness," to the point where "the Lord likes to compare this way with married love. The Lord calls his church his bride; he calls our soul his bride." He speaks of "a love that is so like married love, the love of faithfulness." That means we must "hunt out the idols, to discover them," because they are there and they are well "hidden in our personality, in our way of life." And they make us unfaithful to this love. So it isn't an accident when the apostle James warns: "anyone who is a friend of the world is an enemy of God"; he rebukes us using the term "adulterers," because "anyone who is a friend of the world is an idolater and not faithful to the love of God."

So Jesus proposes "a way of faithfulness," according to an expression that Pope Francis took from one of the letters of the apostle Paul to Timothy: "If you are not faithful to the Lord, he remains faithful, for he can't deny himself. He is all faithfulness. He can't be unfaithful. So great is the love he has for us." Whereas we, "by our small or not so small idolatries, by love for the spirit of the world," can become unfaithful. Faithfulness is the essence of

God who loves us. "So I invite you to pray thus: 'Lord, you are so good, teach me the way to go, so that every day I am less far from the kingdom of God; the way to hunt out all idols.' It's difficult," the pope admitted, "but we must get going."

THE DIFFICULT SCIENCE OF LOVE

Sacred Heart of Jesus

Friday, June 7, 2013
Ezk 34:11–16; Lk 15:3–7

"The science of love has two supports: closeness and tenderness. And Jesus knows this beautiful science well," Pope Francis said this morning, Friday, June 7, when he celebrated Mass on the feast of the Sacred Heart of Jesus in the chapel of St. Martha's Guest House.

Referring to the readings for the day—taken from the book of the prophet Ezekiel (34:11-16), Paul's letter to the Romans (5:5-11), and the Gospel of Luke (5:3-7)—the pope described the feast of the Sacred Heart of Jesus as the "feast of love." Jesus "wanted to show us his heart, that heart which loved so much. That's why we commemorate it today. God's love. God has loved us, loved so much. I'm thinking about what St. Ignatius said to us, to us. He gave two criteria for love. First, love shows more in doing than in speaking. Second, love lies more in giving than in receiving."

These are the two criteria about which "Paul tells us in the second reading: 'While we were still weak, at the right time, Christ died for the ungodly.' Jesus loved us not by speaking but by doing, by his life. And he gave to us, gave to us without receiving anything from us. These two criteria are like the supporting pillars of true love: doing and giving yourself." Explaining the meaning of these two criteria, the Holy Father noted that Jesus' self-giving is depicted well in the story of the Good Samaritan. "Today," he said, "the liturgy shows us God's love in the figure of the shepherd. The responsorial psalm we recited was the beautiful Psalm 22 [23]: The Lord is my shepherd. The Lord also shows himself to his people as a shepherd."

But, asked the pope, "in what way is the Lord a shepherd?" And he explained: "The Lord tells us so many things, but I will only dwell on two of them. The first comes in the book of the prophet Ezekiel: I myself will search for my sheep, and will look them over. Looking them over means that he knows each one of them, by name. Look over. And Jesus tells us the same thing: I know my sheep. Know each one by name. That's how God knows us. He doesn't know us as a group, but one by one. Because," the bishop of Rome continued, "love isn't abstract or a general love for all. It's love for each one. That's how God loves us."

All this translates into closeness: "God," the pope noted, "has come close to us. Let us remember that beautiful passage from Deuteronomy, that loving reproach: What people have had a God so close to them as you?" A God "who comes close through love," he added. "And walks with his people. And that walking with us goes to unimaginable lengths: never would we have thought that the Lord himself would become one of us and walk with us, and stay with us, remain in his church, remain in the Eucharist, remain in his words, remain with the poor, remain with us on the journey. That's closeness. The shepherd close to his flock, to his sheep, whom he knows one by one."

Then turning to the other aspect of God's love, the pope noted that both "the prophet Ezekiel and the gospel speak of it: I will go and seek my lost sheep and bring the one who has strayed back to the sheepfold. I will bind up the injured and cure the sick, I will care for the fat and strong, I will feed them with justice, tenderness. The Lord is familiar with that beautiful science of tenderness. God's tenderness: he doesn't love us only in words; he comes close to us, and by being close to us he gives us his love with all possible tenderness." So closeness and tenderness are "the Lord's two ways of loving, who comes close to us and gives us all his love, even in the littlest things with tenderness." But it's "a strong love. Closeness and tenderness enable us to see the strength of God's love."

"And as for our love—doesn't the Lord tell us: Love as I have loved you?—it too must come close to our neighbor and be tender like that of the Good Samaritan, or like the love the church shows us in the gospel today," added the pope. But how can we give back to the Lord "so many lovely things, that closeness, that tenderness?" Of course, said the pope, "we may say: by loving him, coming close to him, being tender with him. Yes, that's true, but it isn't the most important thing. It may sound like heresy but it's the greatest truth: more difficult than loving God is letting ourselves be loved by him. And that's the way to give back all that love to him: to open our hearts and let ourselves be loved. Let him come close to us, and feel him to be close. Let him be tender and caress us." That, he concluded, "is so difficult: allowing ourselves to be loved by him. And perhaps that's what we should ask for today in this Mass: Lord, I want to love you but teach me the difficult science, the difficult habit of letting myself be loved by you, of feeling you close and feeling your tenderness."

Between Amazement and Memory

Immaculate Heart of Mary

Saturday, June 8, 2013
Tob 12:1, 5–15, 20; Lk 2:41–51

God's word, which just by being heard "causes amazement," must be jealously guarded in the depths of our heart. That is what Pope Francis said this morning, Saturday, June 8, during the Mass celebrated in the chapel of St. Martha's Guest House. In his homily the pope put the stress on amazement. It struck those listening to the twelve-year-old Jesus in the temple when the doctors were questioning him, as Luke's gospel tells us (2:41-51), and Joseph and Mary were also amazed when they found Jesus after three days: "The doctors were full of astonishment," said the pope, "and Joseph and Mary were amazed when they saw Jesus." So the first effect God's word has is amazement, because in it we get a sense of the divine, noted the Holy Father: "And then it gives us joy. But amazement is more than joy. It's a moment when God's word is sown in our heart."

But we shouldn't just experience amazement at the moment when it's aroused by God's word: it's something to take with us throughout our whole life, "something to keep." We must "keep God's word," and said Pope Francis, "the gospel tells us this: his mother kept all these things in her heart." Keeping God's word: an expression, the pope pointed out, often found in the gospel stories: On the night of Jesus' birth, "after the shepherd's visit" Mary "was astonished."

Then Pope Francis reflected on the meaning of "keeping" God's word and he asked: "Do I receive the word, then get a bottle, put the word in the bottle and keep it?" Keeping God's word, he replied, "means opening our hearts" to that word, "as the Earth opens to receive the seed. God's word is a seed that is sown. Some fall by the wayside and the birds come and eat them." This happens when the word isn't kept. It means that "some hearts don't know how to receive it." It also happens that some seeds fall "on stony ground and the seed doesn't manage to put down roots, so it dies." That's when we aren't capable of keeping it because we are inconstant, and when hardships come we forget about it.

"The word also falls on unprepared ground," added the pope, "where there are thorns, and in the end it dies" because "it isn't looked after." But what are the thorns? Jesus tells us himself: "Attachment to riches, vices, all those things. Keeping God's word means receiving it into our hearts," repeated Pope Francis. But it's necessary "to prepare our heart to receive it. Always meditate on what this word is telling us today, looking out for what is happening in life." And that's what Mary did during the flight into Egypt and at the wedding at Cana, when she was asking herself about the meaning of these events. So that's the Christian's task: to receive God's word and to think about what it means today.

"This," said the bishop of Rome, "is a great spiritual work. John Paul II said that, because of this work, Mary had a particular trouble in her heart. Her heart was troubled. But that isn't worry, it's work: to seek what it means at this moment, what the Lord is telling me at this moment." In short, to read "life by God's word: that's what keeping it means." But it also means remembering. "Memory," said the pope, "is keeper of God's word; it helps us to keep it, to remember all that the Lord has done in my life, all the wonders of salvation."

Then the pope asked those present: "So how do we keep God's word today? How do we maintain that amazement" and ensure that the birds don't eat the "seeds" and vices "don't suffocate them?" He answered that it does us good to ask ourselves, in the light of the things that happen in our lives. He urged us to keep the word "in our memory, and also keep it in our hope. Let us ask the Lord," concluded Pope Francis, "for the grace to receive God's word and keep it, and also for the grace to have a heart that is troubled by keeping it."

Doors Open to Consolation

Monday, June 10, 2013
2 Cor 1:1–7; Mt 5:1–12

Why are some people's hearts closed to salvation? This question was the focus of Pope Francis' homily at Mass today,

Monday, June 10, in the chapel of St. Martha's Guest House. A question whose answer and explanation is to be found in fear, because, the pope explained, salvation frightens us. It has an attraction which unleashes the terrors that lie most deeply hidden in our hearts. "We need" salvation but at the same time "we are afraid of it," because, said the Holy Father, "when the Lord comes to save us, we have to give everything" and at that point "he is in command; and that's what we are afraid of." For human beings want to "command"; they want to be "masters" of themselves. And so "salvation doesn't come, the consolation of the Spirit doesn't come."

In the liturgy of the day the gospel passage from Matthew (5:1-12) on the Beatitudes gave the pope the opportunity to reflect on the relation between salvation and freedom. Only the salvation that comes with the consolation of the Spirit, he declared, sets us free; it's "the freedom that is born of the Holy Spirit that saves us, consoles us, gives us life." But in order fully to understand the Beatitudes and what it means "to be poor, to be meek, to be merciful"—all things that "don't seem" to "bring us success"—we must keep "an open heart" and "have tasted the consolation of the Holy Spirit, which is salvation."

What's more, the Beatitudes are "the law of those who have been saved" and have opened their hearts to salvation. "This," he added, "is the law of the free, the freedom of the Holy Spirit." We can "regulate our lives, organize it according to a list of commandments or procedures," but that's a merely human operation, warned Pope Francis. "That's something limited, and in the end it doesn't lead us to salvation," because only "an open heart" can do so.

This gospel says that seeing the crowds, Jesus went up the mountain. "Among the crowds," noted the Holy Father, "there were so many needing salvation. They were the people of God who followed John the Baptist and then the Lord," just because they needed salvation. But there were also others who "went to examine this new doctrine and then to quarrel with Jesus. They didn't have open hearts. Their hearts were closed in upon their own concerns." They were asking what Jesus wanted to change, but "as their hearts were closed, the Lord couldn't change it"; for "unfortunately their hearts were closed."

So the pope invited us to ask the Lord for "the grace to follow him" but not with the freedom of the Pharisees and Sadducees, who became hypocrites because "they wanted to follow him only with human freedom." For that's hypocrisy: "not to let the Spirit change our heart by his salvation. The freedom the Spirit gives us is also a kind of slavery, slavery to the Lord who sets us free. It's a different freedom." On the other hand, our human freedom "is slavery, not to the Lord but to the spirit of the world." Hence the pope's prayer asking for "the grace to open our hearts to the consolation of the Holy Spirit, so that this consolation, which is salvation, may lead us to understand well" the new commandments contained in the gospel of the Beatitudes.

It's no accident that the beginning of Paul's second letter to the Corinthians (1:1-7) in today's liturgy speaks a good "nine times of 'consolation.'" It seems rather excessive, commented the pope. And stressing that Paul "took seven verses to repeat this word 'consolation,'" he asked: "Why does he insist on this? What is this consolation?" The apostle's letter is addressed to Christians who are "young in faith," who "only began on the way of Jesus recently." Paul "insists on that. On the way of Jesus the Father offers us consolation." These Christians "were not all persecuted. They were ordinary people who had found Jesus. And that's a change of life requiring special strength from God, from the Holy Spirit; and that strength is consolation."

What does consolation mean? For Pope Francis "it's the presence of God in our hearts. But for the Lord to come into our hearts we have to open the door." The conversion of these pagans to whom Paul is writing consisted in "opening the door to the Lord." And thus they received "the consolation of the Holy Spirit." In fact salvation is "living in the consolation of Holy Spirit, not living in the consolation of the spirit of the world. That's not salvation, it's sin." On the other hand, salvation is "going ahead and opening our hearts to let in this consolation of the Holy Spirit."

Human beings often run the risk of trying "to negotiate," to take what makes us comfortable, "a bit of this, a bit of that." It's like "making a fruit salad, a bit of Holy Spirit and a bit of the spirit of the world. But with God there are no half measures: you have to choose one thing or the other." In fact, remarked the pope, "the Lord tells us plainly: you cannot serve two masters. You can either serve the Lord or the spirit of the world. You can't mix them." This new law which "the Lord brings us, these new Beatitudes, can only be understood with an open heart. They are understood by the consolation of the Holy Spirit. They can't be understood by human intelligence or by the spirit of the world." We must be open to salvation, otherwise "they can't be understood. They are the new commandments, but if our hearts aren't open to the Holy Spirit they will seem like nonsense."

Signs of Free Giving

Tuesday, June 11, 2013
Acts 11:21–26; 13:1–3; Mt 10:7–13

Poverty and praising God are the two principal coordinates of the church's mission, the "signs" that tell the people of God whether "an apostle lives by giving freely." Pope Francis pointed them out during the Mass this morning, Tuesday, June 11, in the chapel of St. Martha's Guest House.

Taking his cue as usual from the day's readings—Acts of the Apostles (11:21-26; 13:1-3) and Matthew's gospel (10:7-13)— the pope's reflection focused on the subject of giving freely. Because, he explained, "preaching the gospel arises out of giving freely, from amazement at the proffered salvation; and what I have received freely, I must freely give."

This can be seen when Jesus sends out his disciples and gives them instructions for their mission. "They are very simple orders," said the Holy Father, "very simple: don't provide yourself with gold or silver or money," since it will be sufficient to have "belt, travel bag, two tunics, sandals, stick" for the task they have been given. A mission of salvation, Jesus adds, which consists in healing the sick, raising the dead, curing lepers, driving out demons.

It's a mission, said Pope Francis, to bring people closer to the kingdom of God, to give them the good news that the kingdom of God is near; it is at hand. But, he warned, the Lord wants his apostles to have "simplicity" of heart and to be prepared to make room "for the power of God's word." After all, he noted, if they had not had great "faith in the word of God, perhaps they would have done something else," but they would not have proclaimed the gospel.

The key phrase in Christ's orders to his disciples is "freely you have received, so freely give": words containing "the gratuitousness of salvation." Because, explained the pope, "we can't preach, proclaim the kingdom of God without this inner certainty that everything is freely given, everything is grace." St. Augustine said as much: *Quaere causam et non invenies nisi gratiam.* And when we act without leaving room for grace, declared the pope, then "the gospel has no power."

After all, various episodes in the lives of the first apostles witness to the fact that the gospel preaching is given freely. "St. Peter didn't have a bank account, and when he had to pay taxes the Lord sent him to fish in the lake to find the money to pay the tax inside a fish." And when Philip met Queen Candace's minister he didn't think about setting up "an organization to support the gospel"; he didn't negotiate. On the contrary, "he proclaimed, he baptized and he went off." So the good news is spread "by sowing" the word of God. Jesus himself says so: "the kingdom is like the seed God gives. It's a free gift."

Since the beginning of the Christian community there has been "the temptation to seek strength elsewhere that is not freely given." But our only "strength is the gratuitousness of the gospel," repeated the Holy Father, guarding against the risk that the proclamation may seem like proselytizing: "that way you get nowhere," he declared. He quoted his predecessor Benedict XVI, according to whom, "the church doesn't grow by proselytizing" but "by attraction." Because, Pope Francis added, "the Lord has invited us to proclaim, not to make proselytes." And the power of attraction has to come from the witness of those who announce the free gift of salvation. "Everything is grace," he repeated. And among the many signs of this free gift he singled out poverty and praising God.

As to the first, he explained that proclaiming the gospel has to go by way of poverty, by the witness of this poverty. "I have no wealth; my only wealth is the gift I have received from God. This free giving is our wealth." And this is a poverty that "saves us from becoming organizers, entrepreneurs." The pope is aware that "the church's work has to be carried out" and that "some of it is rather complex," but it must be done "with poverty of heart, not as an investment or like an entrepreneur. The church isn't an NGO; it's something else, more important. It's born of a free gift received and proclaimed."

As for the ability to praise, the Holy Father made plain that when an apostle doesn't live in the spirit of giving freely, he also loses the capacity to praise the Lord, "because praising the Lord is essentially giving freely. It's freely given prayer. We don't just ask for things, we also praise." On the other hand, he concluded, "when we find apostles who want to create a rich church, a church without the free gift of praise," that church "grows old, it turns into an NGO, it has no life."

ADOLESCENT PROGRESSIVISM

Wednesday, June 12, 2013
2 COR 3:4–11; MT 5:17–19

At this moment in the church's history she faces two tempta-tions: to go backward because we are afraid of the freedom that comes from the law "fulfilled in the Holy Spirit"; and to give way to an "adolescent progressivism," which is inclined to adopt the most captivating values of the dominant culture. Pope Fran-cis spoke about these two temptations this morning, Wednesday, June 12, commenting on the readings—taken from Paul's second letter to the Corinthians (3:4-11) and Matthew's gospel (5:17-19)—at the Mass in the chapel of St. Martha's Guest House.

First of all, the pope considered the explanations Jesus gave to those who were accusing him of wanting to change the laws of Moses. He reassures them saying: "I have not come to abolish the law but to fulfill it." Because the law, said the Holy Father, "is the fruit of the covenant. The law can't be understood without the covenant. The law is a bit like the way into the covenant," which "began with a promise that afternoon in Eden, then went ahead with Noah's ark, with Moses in the wilderness, and then contin-ued as the law of Israel to do God's will."

That law "is sacred," he added, "because it led the people to God." So it can't be touched. There were those who said that Jesus "changed this law"; but he was trying to make them understand that it was a way that led "to growth" to the full maturity of that law. And he said, "I have come to bring it to fulfillment. The law's continuity toward its maturity is like the bud that 'bursts' and becomes a flower. And Jesus is the expression of the law's fulfillment."

The pope then reaffirmed the role of the Holy Spirit in the transmission of this law. In fact, he explained, "Paul tells us that we have this law of the Spirit through Jesus Christ, because we are not capable of thinking something coming from ourselves; our capacity comes from God. And the law God gives us is a mature law, the law of love, because we have come to the final hour. The apostle John tells his community: Brothers, we have come to the final hour. To the hour of the law's fulfillment. It's the law of the Spirit which sets us free."

However, this is a freedom that in a sense is frightening. "Because," said the pope "it can be confused with that other human freedom." And then "the laws of the Spirit lead us on the way of continual discernment to do God's will": that scares us a bit. But, he said, when we are assailed by that fear we run the risk of succumbing to two temptations. The first is "turning back because we are uncertain. But that interrupts the journey." It's "the temptation to be afraid of freedom, afraid of the Holy Spirit: the Holy Spirit frightens us."

At that point Pope Francis recalled an episode that occurred at the beginning of the 1930s: "A diligent superior of a religious congregation spent many years collecting all the rules of his congregation: what the monks could do and what they could not. Then, when his work was finished, he went to a great Benedictine abbot who was in Rome, to show him his work. The abbot looked at it and said to him: Father, by this you have killed off the charism of your congregation! He had killed off freedom. Because charism bears fruit in freedom and he had blocked it. That isn't life. That congregation couldn't go on living. What happened? Twenty-five years after that masterpiece, no one had seen it and it ended up in a library."

"That is an example of how easy it is to fall into the temptation of going backwards in order to feel safer," explained the bishop of

Rome. But, he added, "full security lies in the Holy Spirit who leads you forward, who gives you confidence, and as Paul says, is more demanding. In fact, Jesus said that until heaven and earth pass away not an iota, not a dot will pass from the law until all is accomplished. So it's more demanding even if it doesn't give us human security, because we can't control the Holy Spirit: that's the problem."

The second temptation was what the pope defined as "adolescent progressivism." But this is not genuine progress: it's a culture that goes on, from which we don't manage to detach ourselves and from which we take the laws and values we like best, just as adolescents do. In the end we risk slithering "as a car slithers on an icy road and goes off track."

According to the pope that is a recurrent temptation at this moment in the church's history. "We can't go backward," said the pope, "and slide off track."

The road to follow is this: "The law continues in full, without cutting any of it out: as the seed ends up as a flower, as fruit. The road is the way of freedom in the Holy Spirt, who sets us free, in continual discernment of God's will, to go forward along this road, without going backward," and without backsliding. "This is not a call to bring back Joachim of Fiore," said the pope. And he concluded: "Let us ask the Holy Spirit to give us life, to lead us forward, to bring the law to full maturity, that law which sets us free."

THE TONGUE CAN KILL TOO

Thursday, June 13, 2013
2 COR 3:5—4:1, 3–6; MT 5:20–26

Anger and insulting our brother can kill. Pope Francis reminded us of this in the Mass this morning, Thursday, June

13, in the chapel of St. Martha's Guest House. He was commenting on the gospel passage of the day's liturgy (Matthew 5:20-26), where we are told that anyone who is angry with his brother will be liable to judgment.

Recalling St. John, who says that anyone who expresses resentment or hatred against a brother is really already killing him at heart, the pope stressed the need to enter the logic of perfection, that is, to "review our conduct." Of course, he said, addressing the faithful in Spanish, this reminds us of the business of "discrediting our brother through our own inner passion. In practice this means insulting." However, the pope noted ironically how widespread recourse is to insults "in the Latin tradition" with "marvelous creativity, since we invent one after another."

As long as "the epithet is friendly, just let it go," admitted the pope. But "the problem arises when there comes another, more offensive epithet." "Then," he said, "we go on to qualify it with a series of definitions that are not exactly evangelical." In practice, he explained, an insult is a way of putting down the other person. In fact, "we don't need to go to a psychologist to realize that when we put someone down, belittle them, it's because we are unable to grow up and need to make the other person small, so that we feel we are somebody. These are ugly ploys." On the other hand, the pope recalled, Jesus says quite simply: "Don't speak ill of anyone, don't belittle them, don't discredit them. Basically we are all walking along the same road."

This reflection was inspired by the gospel passage for the day, which, the pope recalled, continues with the Sermon on the Mount. Jesus, he said, "proclaims a new law. Jesus is the new Moses, promised by God: I will give a new Moses… And he announces the new law. That's the Beatitudes. The Sermon on the Mount." As Moses proclaimed the law on Mount Sinai, so Jesus has come to say "that he hasn't come to abolish the previous law but to fulfill it, to take it forward, to bring it to maturity," so that it reaches its fullness. Jesus, continued the pope, "makes very clear that he hasn't come to abolish the law until the last dot and the last comma of the law is fulfilled." So he has come to explain what this new law is: "Of course, he was making an adjustment; he was adapting it to new legal parameters." Certainly it's a reform; and yet "it's a reform without a break, a reform with continuity: from the seed to the fruit."

When Jesus makes this speech, the pope went on, he begins with the sentence "Your righteousness must be more than what you are seeing now, the righteousness of the scribes and Pharisees." And if this righteousness doesn't "exceed that, you will be lost, you will not enter the kingdom of heaven." So "anyone who embarks on Christian life, anyone who undertakes to follow that way, is subject to greater demands than anyone else." And here he made clear: "They don't have greater advantages, no! They have greater demands put on them." And Jesus himself mentions some of them, among others, "the requirement to live together," and then also speaks about "negative relationships with our brothers." Jesus' words, stressed the pope, offer no way of escape: "You have heard that it was said in the past: you shall not murder. Anyone who murders shall be liable to judgment. But I say to you that anyone who is angry with a brother deserves to be condemned, and anyone who insults him will be liable to judgment."

As to insults, noted the pope, Jesus is even more radical and "goes much further." Because, he says, even when "you begin to feel something negative in your heart" against a brother and express it "with an insult, a curse, or with anger, there is something wrong. You must be converted, you must change."

Then Pope Francis reminded us of the apostle James who says "a boat is steered by its helm and a person by their tongue." So, the Holy Father stressed, if someone "isn't capable of ruling their tongue, they are lost." It's a point of human weakness. It goes a long way back, because "that natural aggressiveness that Cain had toward Abel is repeated throughout history. It's not that we are wicked but we are weak and we are sinners." That's why, he continued, "it's much easier to settle a situation with an insult, with slander, with libel, than to settle it in a good way, as Jesus says." But Jesus is clear when he invites us to make up with our enemy and come to an understanding, so that we don't end up in court. And he goes even further. "If you go to praise your Father," added the pope, "and when you go to offer a gift at the altar you remember that you have a problem with your brother, first resolve the problem."

In conclusion, the pope asked the Lord for the grace for all to "pay a bit more attention to our tongue, to what we say about others." Doubtless, it's "a small penance, but it bears good fruit." It's true it requires sacrifice and strength, since it's much easier to enjoy "the taste of a juicy comment against someone." In the long run when we abstain, "this hunger does us good." Hence the need to ask the Lord for the grace "to adapt our lives to this new law, which is the law of gentleness, the law of love, the law of peace." We should start by "curbing our tongue a bit, curbing the comments we make about others or the explosions that lead us to insult them, to lose our temper."

TRUE CHRISTIAN HUMILITY

Friday, June 14, 2013
2 COR 4:7–15; MT 5:27–32

Without humility, without the ability to recognize our own sins and human weakness publicly, we can't attain salvation or claim to proclaim Christ or be his witnesses. That's also true for priests: Christians must always remember that the wealth of grace, God's gift, is a treasure kept in "clay pots" to make plain God's extraordinary power, which no one can appropriate "for their own personal *curriculum vitae.*"

Once again Pope Francis invited us to reflect on the subject of Christian humility, during the Mass this morning, Friday, June 14, in the chapel of St. Martha's Guest House. The pope's meditation focused on the readings for the day—from Paul's second letter to the Corinthians (4:7-15) and Matthew's gospel. He compared the image of "Jesus' beauty, Jesus' strength, the salvation Jesus brings us," about which the apostle Paul speaks on another page, with that of the "clay pots," in which the treasure of the faith is contained.

Christians are like the clay pots; they are fragile because they are sinners. Nevertheless, stressed the pope, there is a dialogue between "us poor clay pots" and "the power of the savior Jesus Christ." It's "the dialogue of salvation." But, he warned, when this dialogue adopts a tone of self-justification it means that something isn't working and there is no salvation. Paul teaches the way to go, continued Pope Francis. In fact, "He spoke so often of his sins, it was almost like a refrain: 'I tell you I was a persecutor of the church... I persecuted...' There is always the memory of sin in him. He feels he is a sinner." But "he doesn't say, 'I was a sinner, but now I'm a saint.'"

Among us something else happens. The pope explained by comparing it with the behavior of the apostle Paul. "Each time Paul tells us about his service record—'I've done this, I've done that, I've preached'—he also speaks of what has gone with it, his vademecum, that is, his weaknesses, his sins. But we always have the temptation to announce the record and to disguise the vademecum a little, so that it's less visible. That won't do."

Christian humility goes the way of the apostle. That model of humility applies also "to us priests, us clergy. If we only boast about our record and nothing else, said the bishop of Rome, we will end up making a mistake. We can't "proclaim Jesus Christ as savior, because deep down we don't feel it." "We must be humble—but with real humility, with name and surname: 'I am a sinner, because, because, because.' As Paul does." We must acknowledge that we are sinners, in particular ways, and not present ourselves with a false image, "a holy picture face." And to make it more vivid, Pope Francis used a Piedmontese expression: "to pull a munia quacia [a 'still water' face], to act the innocent. That innocence isn't real, it's merely the appearance of it."

But, said the pope, the humility of priests, Christian humility, must "be real: 'I am a clay pot because, because, because.' And when Christians fail to make this confession, to themselves, before the church, something is wrong." Above all, he added, "they can't understand the beauty of the salvation brought to us by Jesus Christ: that treasure."

"Brothers and sisters," he said, "we have a treasure: the treasure of Jesus Christ the savior, the cross of Jesus Christ, that treasure we boast about." But let us not forget "also to confess our sins," because only then "does the dialogue actually become Christian and Catholic. Because Jesus Christ's salvation is real and actual. Jesus Christ didn't save us by an idea, by an intellectual program. He saved us by his flesh, by his real flesh and blood. He lowered himself and became man, he became flesh to the end." We can only understand and receive such a treasure if we become clay pots.

In conclusion, the pope put forward the image of the Samaritan woman. That woman who talked to Jesus went off quickly when the disciples arrived. "And what does she say to the townspeople? 'I've found someone who told me everything I've ever done.'" Someone who had made her understand the meaning of her being a clay pot. That woman had found Jesus Christ the savior and when she came to proclaim him, she did so by speaking first about her own sins. She explained that she had asked Jesus:

"Do you know who I am? And he told me everything."

"I believe," the pope concluded, "that this woman will be in heaven." And to account for his certainty he cited [Italian poet Alessandro] Manzoni: "'But I've never found that the Lord began a miracle without completing it.' And that miracle which he began he surely completed in heaven."

CHRISTIAN HASTE

Saturday, June 15, 2013
2 COR 5:14–21; MT 5:33–37

Christian life should always be restless, never soporific and certainly not "terminal care to keep us quiet till we get to heaven." We need to act like St. Paul and "bear witness to the message of true reconciliation," without bothering too much about statistics or making converts: "it's mad but it's beautiful" because "it's the scandal of the cross." The pope spoke again about reconciliation and apostolic zeal in his homily at the Mass celebrated this morning, Saturday, June 15, in the chapel of St. Martha's Guest House.

As usual the pope based his reflection on the readings for the day, in particular the second letter of St. Paul to the Corinthians (5:14-21), "rather a special passage," he said, "because it seems as if Paul sets out in fourth gear. He's in a hurry, he goes at a certain speed. The love of Christ possesses us, drives us, presses us on. And that's the hurry Paul is in: when he sees Christ's love he can't stay still." So St. Paul is really a man in a hurry, "breathlessly wanting to tell us something important: he speaks of the 'yes' Jesus said, the work of reconciliation Jesus did and also the work of reconciliation" of Christ and the apostle.

Pope Francis also pointed out that in this text of Paul's "the word reconciliation is repeated five times. Five times, like a refrain," to say clearly that "God has reconciled us to himself in Christ." St. Paul "also speaks strongly and tenderly when he says I am an ambassador in Christ's name." Then as his letter goes on, Paul seems almost to throw himself on his knees to implore: "I beg you in Christ's name: let yourselves be reconciled to God." It's as if he said "lower your guard" to let yourself be reconciled with him.

"Paul's haste, Paul's hurry," the pope went on to say, "reminds me of Mary when, after she had received the angel's message, she set out in haste to help her cousin. It's the haste of the Christian message. And here the message is indeed a message of reconciliation." The meaning of reconciliation is not simply bringing different, distant parties together. "True reconciliation is that God in Christ took on our sins and became sin for us. And when we go to confession, for example, it's not just telling our sin and God forgiving us. We find Jesus Christ and tell him this is yours and I am making you become sin again. And he likes that, because his mission was to become sin for us, in order to set us free."

And that "is the mystery that drove Paul onward with apostolic zeal, because it's something so wonderful: God's love that delivered his Son to death for me. When Paul faces this truth he says: but he loved me, he went to his death for me. That's the mystery of reconciliation." Christian life, explained the pope, "grows on this foundation, and we debase it somewhat" when we reduce it to the dictum that "Christians must do this and believe that." What matters is getting "to this truth that moves us, to this love that is within Christian life: the Father's love reconciling the world in Christ. It's God who reconciles the world to himself in Christ, not counting our sins against us and entrusting us with the word of reconciliation. Christ has reconciled us. And that's the Christian attitude, Christian peace."

Philosophers "say that peace is the tranquillity of order. Everything ordered, everything tranquil. But that isn't Christian peace. Christian peace," insisted Pope Francis, "is a restless peace; it's not a tranquil peace. It's a restless peace that sets out to bring this message of reconciliation. Christian peace drives us forward and is the beginning, the root of apostolic zeal."

According to Pope Francis, "apostolic zeal doesn't mean going ahead to make converts and statistics: this year the number of Christians has grown in such and such a country, Christian movements. Statistics are good, they help, but making converts isn't what God wants most from us. What the Lord wants from us," said the pope, "is to proclaim reconciliation, which is the nucleus of his message: Christ became sin for me and sinners are there, in his body, in his soul. This is mad but it's beautiful: it's the truth. This is the scandal of the cross."

The pope concluded his homily by asking for the grace for "the Lord to give us this haste to proclaim Jesus; give us Christian wisdom, which flowed from his side, pierced by love." And "that he may convince us that Christian life isn't terminal care to keep us quiet until heaven. Christian life is on the road, living life, with Paul's haste. Christ's love possesses us, drives us, presses us. With the emotion we feel when we see a God who loves us."

The Christian All or Nothing

Monday, June 17, 2013
2 Cor 6:1–10; Mt 5:38–42

"The 'nothing' is always the seed of war, because it's the seed of selfishness. And the 'all' is Jesus, who is the great one." The gentleness and kindness that distinguish Christians is based on an understanding of those two opposites. That's what Pope

Francis said this morning, Monday, June 17, during the Mass celebrated in the chapel of St. Martha's Guest House.

Commenting on the readings for the day—taken from the second letter of St. Paul to the Corinthians (6:1-10) and Matthew's gospel (5:38-42)—the pope dwelled on the meaning of what he described as "a classic" of the gospel teachings, that is, the meaning of what Jesus says about the slap on the cheek, to which the Christian responds by turning the other cheek. That, said the pope, goes against the world's logic, whereby an offence is answered with an equal action against it, because "we have to defend ourselves, we have to fight, we have to defend our position. And if they hit us, we'll hit back twice; that's how we defend ourselves. That's the normal logic, isn't it?"

But Jesus goes further and tells us that when we have received the slap, the pope explained, we have to pause with the other, give him time. And if he asks for something, we must give him much more. That is Jesus' law: "the justice he brings is another kind of justice, completely different from an eye for an eye and a tooth for a tooth." The Holy Father then drew attention to the phrase with which Paul concludes this passage read during the liturgy: "Paul gives us a word that may help us understand the meaning of the slap on the cheek and other such things. In fact he concludes by saying 'as people having nothing yet possessing everything.'"

And this was the pair of opposites the bishop of Rome invited us to reflect on: nothing and everything. "This," he said, "I believe is the key to interpreting Jesus' words, the key to interpreting rightly the justice Jesus demands of us, a righteousness that is greater than that of the scribes and Pharisees." How can we resolve the tension between nothing and everything? The "everything" constitutes Christian security: "We are sure we possess everything, everything with the salvation of Jesus Christ. And Paul was so convinced of this that he says: But for me what matters is Jesus Christ, the rest doesn't matter; for me the rest can be thrown away. The all is Jesus Christ. Others things are nothing to the Christian. But for the spirit of the world, the all is things: wealth, vanity, importance" and "the nothing is Jesus."

This, the pope explained, is expressed by saying if a Christian is asked for ten, "he must give a hundred," because "for him the all is Jesus Christ." That is "the secret of Christian kindness, which always goes together with gentleness. The Christian is someone who enlarges his heart by this kindness. He has the all, which is Jesus Christ; the other things are nothing. They are good, useful, but when they are compared the Christian always chooses the all," which is Jesus.

Gentleness and kindness. Of course, "living like that isn't easy," the pope recognized, "because they really give you slaps and on both cheeks." But "the Christian is gentle, the Christian is kind. He enlarges his heart. And when we find small-hearted Christians," it means that they live "with a selfishness masked as Christianity." For "Jesus advised us: 'Seek first God's kingdom and his justice and the rest will come of its own accord.' The kingdom of God is everything; the rest is secondary, not the main thing." And all the mistakes made by Christians, "all the mistakes made by the church, all our mistakes arise from this: when we tell the nothing it is the all and the all seems not to count," warned the pope.

Following Jesus, he said, "isn't easy. It's not easy but it's not difficult either, because along the road of love the Lord enables us to walk on. And that same Lord enlarges our hearts." But when we are more inclined to follow the nothing, then "disputes arise in families, between friends, in society. Including those disputes that end in war." The "nothing is always the seed of war, because it's the seed of selfishness." And the "all is Jesus, who is the great one." The grace invoked by the pope was that the Lord "may enlarge our hearts and make us humble, gentle and kind, because we have everything in him." That will keep us from creating "daily problems about nothing."

LOVING OUR ENEMIES

Tuesday, June 18, 2013
2 COR 8:1–9; MT 5:43–48

Loving our enemies, those who persecute us and make us suffer, is difficult, and it's not even "a good bargain," because it makes us poorer. Nevertheless, this is the way Jesus pointed to and he himself followed for our salvation. Pope Francis spoke about this in his homily at the Mass celebrated this morning, Tuesday, June 18, in the chapel of St. Martha's Guest House.

During the homily the pope recalled that the liturgy for the present few days invites us to reflect on the parallelisms between "the old law and the new, the law of Mount Sinai and the law of the Beatitudes in the Sermon on the Mount." Discussing the readings for the day—taken from the second letter of St. Paul to the Corinthians (8:1-9) and Matthew's gospel (5:43-48)—the Holy Father dwelled on the difficulty of loving our enemies, and, wondering how it's possible to forgive, he added: "We too, all of us, have enemies, all of us. Some enemies are weak, some are strong. And so often we too become enemies of others; we don't like them. Jesus tells us we must love our enemies."

This is not an easy task and, as a rule, "we think that Jesus is asking too much of us. We think, 'Let's leave it to the holy nuns, or to some other holy soul!'" But that's not the right attitude. "Jesus," the pope recalled, "says that this has to be done, otherwise you become like the tax collectors, like the pagans, and you're not Christians." In the face of so many human dramas, he admitted, it's difficult to make this choice. For how can we love "those who decide to bomb and kill so many people? How can we love those who, for love of money, prevent medicines from reaching people who need them, old people for example, and let them die?" And again: "How can we love those who seek only their own interest, their own power and do so much harm?"

"I don't know how it can be done," said the bishop of Rome. But "Jesus tells us two things: First, look at the Father. God our Father makes the sun rise on good and bad people, makes the rain fall on the just and the unjust. Our Father doesn't say to the sun in the morning: 'Today give light to these and these, but not to those; let them stay in the dark!' He says: 'Give them all light.' His love is for everybody; his love is a gift for everybody, good and bad. And Jesus ends with this advice: 'So you must be perfect just as your heavenly Father is perfect.'" So Jesus tells us to imitate the Father in "that perfect love. He forgives his enemies. He does everything to forgive them. Remember how tenderly Jesus receives Judas in the Garden of Gethsemane," when some of his disciples are thinking of revenge.

"Revenge," said the pope, "is such a good meal when it's eaten cold," so that is why we wait for the right moment to get it. "But that's not Christian," he repeated. "Jesus asks us to love our enemies. How can this be done? Jesus tells us: pray, pray for your enemies." Prayer works miracles, and works not only when we are in our enemies' presence; it works when we are nursing a grievance, "some little enmity." Then we need to pray, because "it's as if the Lord came with soothing oil and prepared our hearts for peace."

"But," added the pope, turning to those present, "now I want to leave you with a question that each of you can answer in your own heart: Do I pray for my enemies? Do I pray for those who don't like me? If we say yes, I say to you: go ahead, pray more, because that is a good way. If the answer is no, the Lord says: You poor thing! You too are an enemy of other people. And you need to pray that the Lord changes their hearts."

The pope then warned against attitudes justifying revenge in accordance with the level of the offence received, of the evil done by others: revenge, that is, based on the principle "an eye for an eye, a tooth for a tooth." We must look again at the example of Jesus: "For you know the grace about which the apostle Paul speaks today: that though he was rich, yet for your sakes he became poor, so that by his poverty you might become rich. It's true: love for our enemies makes us poor, like Jesus, who came and lowered himself and made himself poor." Perhaps it isn't a "good bargain," added the pope, or at least, it isn't according to the world's logic. However, "it's the way taken by God, the way taken by Jesus," to win for us the grace that has made us rich.

This "is the mystery of salvation: by forgiveness, by love for our enemies we become poorer. But that poverty is a fertile seed for others, just as Jesus' poverty became grace for all of us, salvation. Let's think about our enemies, those who don't like us. It would be a good thing if we offered Mass for them, if we offered Jesus' sacrifice for those who don't love us. And also for ourselves, that the Lord may give us this wisdom that is so difficult but also so fine and makes us like his Son, who lowered himself and became poor in order to enrich us out of his poverty."

The Grace of Joy and Kindness

Wednesday, June 19, 2013
2 Cor 9:6–11; Mt 6:1–6, 16–18

"Intellectuals without insight, moralists without kindness, museum pieces without beauty": these are the three sorts of "hypocrites whom Jesus so often reproached." Pope Francis spoke about them at the Mass on Wednesday morning, June 19, in the chapel of St. Martha's Guest House, dwelling on the hypocrisy that is also to be found in the church and the harm it does.

During the homily the pope recalled that "the Lord speaks about hypocrisy several times in the gospel" and "against hypocrites." He pointed out the three most important episodes. The first was when the Pharisees wanted to test Jesus, by asking whether it was lawful to pay taxes to Caesar (Matthew 22:15-22). The second was when the Sadducees presented him with the case of the woman who was widowed seven times (Matthew 22:24-33). For the pope these two episodes represent a particular category of hypocrites: those who "went by way of casuistry" and thus "wanted to make Jesus fall into a trap."

The third time when reference is made to hypocrites—"even more strongly," said the Holy Father—is in chapter 23 of Matthew's gospel, when Christ turns on the scribes and Pharisees with a reprimand that the pope summed up in this way: "Hypocrites, you who don't enter the kingdom of heaven, don't let others in either; hypocrites who make your phylacteries wide and your fringes long." For Pope Francis this kind of hypocrite belongs to a second type: those who go by way of rules, by "so many rules and regulations that God's word becomes unfruitful"; and "also by way of vanity," of phylacteries and fringes. "They become vain and end up becoming ridiculous," he remarked.

In short, the Holy Father said, "the first lot are hypocrites of casuistry; they are casuistic intellectuals," who "don't have the intelligence to find or to explain God." They are "stuck in casuistry: so far you can, so far you can't." Applying it to the present, he said, they are "talentless Christian intellectuals." The second lot are hypocrites of rules and regulations, who "who lead the people of God to a dead end. They are moralists without goodness. They don't know what goodness is. They are moralists: you must do

this and this and this… They pile on the rules and regulations."
But "without goodness." They deck themselves with "fine clothes,
so many things to pretend to be majestic, perfect," and yet "they
have no sense of beauty. They are museum pieces."

But Pope Francis warned the story isn't finished. And in the
day's gospel (Matthew 6:1-6, 16-18), the Lord speaks about another kind of hypocrite, holy hypocrites. This kind, he explained,
is the worst, because it smacks of the sin against the Holy Spirit.
"The Lord speaks about fasting, prayer, and almsgiving: the three
pillars of Christian piety, of the inner conversion that the church
proposes for all of us during Lent. And here there are hypocrites
who parade their fasting, almsgiving, and praying. I think that
when hypocrisy reaches that point in our relationship with God,
we are getting close to the sin against the Holy Spirit. These people know nothing about beauty, they know nothing about love,
they know nothing about truth; they are small and mean."

However, all is not lost. Help toward taking the opposite road
comes from what Paul tells us in the first reading (2 Corinthians
9:6-11). In fact, the Holy Father continued, "the apostle speaks to
us about generosity, about joy. We are all tempted to be hypocritical.
All of us. All Christians. But we all also have grace, the grace that
comes from Jesus Christ, the grace of joy, the grace of kindness, generosity." Well, if "hypocrisy doesn't know what joy is, doesn't know
what generosity is, doesn't know what kindness is," Paul points us
toward a different way, a way "of joy, of generosity, of kindness."

So then Pope Francis spoke out against "hypocrisy in the
church." "What a lot of harm it does to all of us!" he exclaimed.
Because "all of us are capable of becoming hypocrites." The pope
invited us to think of Jesus, "who tells us to pray in secret, and
when we fast to put oil on our head and wash our face, and not
to sound a trumpet before us when we give alms." Here, he said,
quoting Jesus' parable related in Luke's gospel (18:9-14), in our
praying we can learn from that beautiful image of the tax col-

lector: Lord have pity on me, a sinner. And this, he urged, is the prayer we should all say every day, aware that we are sinners, with actual sins, not theoretical ones.

And the same parable shows us another attitude, which is to be avoided, that of the Pharisee, whom the pope stigmatized thus: "But Lord, I do this; I am in such and such an association… It won't do." On the contrary, he concluded, "let us ask the Lord to save us from all hypocrisy and to give us the grace of love, generosity, kindness, and joy."

Praying the Our Father

Thursday, June 20, 2013
2 Cor 11:1–11; Mt 6:7–15

There's no need to waste a lot of words when you pray: the Lord knows what we want to say to him. The important thing is that the first word of our prayer should be "Father." Pope Francis repeated Jesus' advice to the apostles this morning, Thursday, June 20, during the Mass he celebrated in the chapel of St. Martha's Guest House.

The pope repeated Jesus' recommendations at the time when he taught the Our Father to the apostles, according to the account in Matthew's gospel (6:7-15). Briefly, the pope said, in order to pray there is no need to make a noise about it or to believe it's necessary to spend a lot of words. We shouldn't trust in the noise of the world that Jesus called "sounding a trumpet," or "let ourselves be seen on a fast day." In order to pray, he repeated, there is no need for the noise of vanity. Jesus said that was the way pagans behaved.

Pope Francis went further, saying that prayer is not a magic formula: "Prayer isn't a magic formula, you can't work magic by

prayer." As he often does, he spoke about his own personal experience. He said he had never resorted to witch doctors who
promise magic, but that he knew what went on in meetings of
this kind: they spend so many words to get "a cure or something
else" with the help of magic. But, he warned, "that's pagan."

So how should we pray? It was Jesus who taught us how. "He
says that the Father who is in heaven 'knows what we need even
before we ask him.'" So let our first word be "'Father.' That's the
key to prayer. Without saying, without feeling that word you can't
pray," explained the bishop of Rome. And he asked: "Who should
I pray to? Almighty God? He is too distant. I don't feel him,
neither did Jesus. Who do I pray to? The Cosmic God? That's
quite usual these days, isn't it? Praying to the cosmic God. That
polytheistic mode comes with a superficial culture."

But instead, we need to "pray to the Father," the one who created us, "who gave you life, you and me," as an individual person, the pope explained. He is the Father "who goes with you
on your journey," the one who "knows your whole life, all of it";
the one who knows "what is good and what isn't so good. He
knows everything." But that's still not enough: "If we don't begin
our prayer with that word, not just spoken by our lips but in our
hearts, we can't pray like Christians."

And to explain the meaning of the word "Father" even better,
the pope recalled the trusting attitude with which Isaac—"that
twenty-two year old boy was no fool," stressed Pope Francis—
turned to his father when he realized there was no lamb for the
sacrifice and the suspicion arose in him that he himself was to be
the sacrificial victim: "He had to ask and the Bible tells us that he
said: 'Father, there is no lamb.' But he trusted the one who stood
beside him. He was his father. So he passed his worry that 'maybe
I'm the lamb?' into his father's heart."

That's what happened too in the parable of the son who
squandered his inheritance, "but then went home and said: 'Fa-

ther, I have sinned.' And the key to all prayer: to feel loved by a father"; and we have "a Father, who is very close, who folds us in his arms," and with whom we can leave all our cares because "he knows what we need."

But, asked the pope, "is he just my Father?" And he answered: "No, he's our Father, because I'm not his only child. None of us is. If I can't be a brother, it will be difficult for me to become the child of this Father, because surely he's also Father to others, my brothers and sisters." Hence it follows, he continued, "if I'm not at peace with my brothers, I can't call him Father. And that explains why, after teaching us the Our Father, Jesus immediately says, 'If you forgive others their trespasses, your heavenly Father will also forgive you; but if you don't forgive others, neither will your Father forgive you your trespasses.'"

So it's a question of forgiveness. But "it's so difficult to forgive others," repeated the Holy Father; it's really difficult because we always have within us resentment for what they have done to us, for the wrong we have suffered. We can't pray if we still feel rancor against our enemies. "That," stressed the pope, "is difficult. Yes, it's difficult, it's not easy." But, he concluded, "Jesus has promised us the Holy Spirit. It is he who teaches us within, in our heart, how to say 'Father' and how to say 'our,'" and how to say it "making peace with all our enemies."

IN SEARCH OF THE REAL TREASURE

Friday, June 21, 2013
2 Cor 11:18, 21–30; Mt 6:19–23

"Love, kindness, service, patience, goodness, tenderness" are "the most beautiful treasures," about which Pope Francis spoke this morning, Friday, June 21, during the Mass in the chapel of St. Martha's Guest House.

As usual the pope based his reflection on the readings for the day. In the passage from Matthew's gospel (6:19-23), he focused particularly on the "common thread" between the terms "treasure, heart, and light" and hoped that "the Lord might change our hearts to seek the real treasure and thus become people of light rather than people of darkness."

The first thing to do, explained the Holy Father, is to ask yourself: "What is my treasure?" And of course it can't be riches, seeing that the Lord says, "Don't store up for yourselves treasures on Earth, because in the end they are lost." Besides, stressed the pope, "they are risky treasures, which get lost"; and they are also "treasures we must leave behind; we can't take them with us. I've never seen a moving van behind a funeral procession," he commented. So, he asked, what is the treasure we can take with us at the end of our life on Earth? The answer is simple: "You can take what you've given, only that. But you can't take what you have saved up for yourself." These are things that can be stolen by thieves, or things that can be ruined, or things that will be taken over by your heirs. Whereas "that treasure we have given to others" during our lives, we will take with us after death "and that will be 'our merit,'" or rather, he said, "the merit of Jesus Christ in us." It's the only thing "that the Lord lets us take with us." Jesus himself said so plainly to the doctors of the law who were boasting about the beauty of the Jerusalem temple: "Not one stone will remain upon another." The same goes "for our treasures, those that depend on wealth, on human power."

The Holy Father noted that Jesus doesn't just confine himself to criticism. He goes a step further and adds: "Where your treasure is, there will your heart be also." We need to consider that "the Lord made us to seek him, to find him, to grow. But if our treasure isn't close to the Lord, doesn't come from the Lord, our heart grows restless." For example? "Like so many people, we too are restless," said the pope, "to get something or somewhere. And in the end our heart grows tired, it becomes lazy, a loveless heart." Vividly the pope defined "weariness of heart. We think: What have I got? A tired heart, which wants to settle for just three or four things, with a fat bank account? Or have I got a restless heart, ever seeking the things of the Lord?" Hence the invitation "always to keep" that restlessness of heart. Because on our own we can't do much; the Lord must help us, he who promised: "I will turn your heart of stone into a heart of flesh, a human heart." And since the Lord has promised, we can ask for the grace: "Lord, change my heart." On the other hand, "the Lord can do nothing," warned Pope Francis, "if my heart is attached to an earthly treasure, a selfish treasure, a treasure of hate," one of those treasures from which "wars come."

The final part of Jesus' reflection refers to the expression "The body's lamp is the eye," or rather "the eye is the heart's intention." Consequently, for the pope, "if your eye is simple, if it comes from a loving heart, a heart that seeks the Lord, a humble heart, then your whole body will be light. But if your eye is bad, then your whole body will be dark." So the Holy Father told those present to ask themselves how our judgment is on things: "light or dark? Are we people of light or people of darkness? What's important is how we judge things: by the light that comes from the real treasure in our heart? Or by the darkness of a heart of stone?" We could find an answer in the witness of St. Louis Gonzaga, the young Jesuit whose liturgical feast is today. The pope invited: "We can ask for the grace of a new heart from this brave young man," who never held back "in the service of others," so that he gave his life caring for those stricken with the plague. So the Holy Father urged us to ask in prayer that "the Lord may change our heart. And may the Lord make all those stony bits of our heart human, with the yearning to go ahead and seek him and come closer to him." Because, he concluded, only the Lord can save us "from the treasures that can't help us find him or serve others."

THE PILLARS OF CHRISTIAN SALVATION

Saturday, June 22, 2013
2 COR 12:1–10; MT 6:24–34

Riches and the cares of the world make us forgetful of the past, confused in the present, uncertain about the future. That is to say, they make us lose sight of the three pillars upon which Christian salvation history rests: a Father who chose us in the past, who has made us a promise for our future, and to whom we have given an answer confirming a covenant with him in the present. That was the gist of Pope Francis' reflection during the Mass celebrated this morning, Saturday, June 22, in St. Martha's Guest House.

The pope's homily went on to talk about the account in Matthew's gospel (6:24-34), which speaks of Jesus' advice to his disciples: "when he says, 'No one can serve two masters because he will love the one and hate the other. You cannot serve God and money.' And then he continues: 'Therefore I tell you, do not worry about your life, what you will eat or what you will drink.'" "We get help to understand this," said the pope, "from chapter 13 of St. Matthew's gospel, which gives Jesus' explanation to the disciples of the parable of the sower. He says the seed that falls among thorns is choked. But what chokes it? Jesus says: 'riches and the cares of the world.' We can see that Jesus had a clear idea about this."

So "riches and the cares of the world choke the word of God," said the pope. "They don't allow it to grow. And the word dies because it isn't looked after, it's choked. In that case riches and the cares of the world are looked after but not the word of God."

In his explanation to his disciples, Jesus introduces the element of time, the pope pointed out. Then he asked: "What do riches do to us, what do the cares of the world do?" "They simply take us out of time," he replied. He went on to explain: "Our whole life is based on three pillars, one in the past, one in the present, and the other in the future. That's clear in the Bible: the pillar of the past is our election. The Lord has chosen us. Each of us can say: 'The Lord has chosen me, loved me, called me to come, and he has chosen me in baptism to follow a way, the Christian way.'" The future is the promise Jesus made to humanity: "He has chosen me," the bishop of Rome continued, "to go toward a promise; he gave us a promise." Finally, the present "is our answer to this good God, who has chosen me, given me a promise, and offers me a covenant; and I form a covenant with him."

So election, promise, and covenant are the three pillars of salvation history. But it may sometimes happen that "when our heart comes into what Jesus has explained to us," added the Holy Father, "it cuts out time. It cuts out the past, it cuts out the future and becomes confused in the present." That happens because someone "who is attached to riches isn't interested in the past, or in the future; he has everything. Wealth is an idol. He has no need of a past, of a promise, of an election, or of a future or of anything. What he's worried about is what may happen"; so "he cuts off his link with the future," which for him becomes "futurible" [potential or speculative]. But it certainly doesn't direct him toward a promise, so he remains confused, alone. "That's why Jesus tells us: 'Either God or riches, either the kingdom of God and his justice or the cares of the world.' He simply invites us to walk along the road of that great gift he has given us: to be his chosen ones. By baptism we are chosen in love," stated the pope.

"We don't cut off from the past; we have a Father who has set us on our way. And we are also glad about the future because we are going toward a promise and we aren't bogged down in cares. The Lord is faithful, he doesn't deceive us. So let's walk on," urged the pope. As for the present, "let's do what we can in our actual daily lives, without illusions and without forgetting that we have a Father in the past who has chosen us."

So, Pope Francis added, "let's remember well: the seed that falls among thorns is choked; it's choked by riches and the cares of the world," two things that make us forget the past and the future. So then, "we have a Father, but we live as if we didn't" and we have an uncertain future. In this way even the present "is something that doesn't work." But for that very reason, the pope reassured us, we "should trust in the Lord who says: 'Don't worry; seek first the kingdom of God and his justice. All the rest will come.'" Concluding his homily, the pope urged us to ask the Lord for the grace not to make the mistake of giving weight to worldly cares and to the idolatry of riches, but always to remember that "we have a Father who has chosen us and who promises us something good." So we must "go toward that promise, taking the present as it comes."

The Example of John the Baptist

Monday, June 24, 2013
Is 49:1–6; Lk 1:57–66, 80

A church inspired by the figure of John the Baptist: that "exists to proclaim, to voice a word, word of her bridegroom who is the Word" and "to proclaim this word to the point of martyrdom" at the hands of "the proudest on Earth." This was what Pope Francis proposed during the Mass celebrated in the chapel of St. Martha's Guest House this morning, Monday, June 24, the feast of the birthday of John the Baptist, whom the church venerates as "the greatest man born of woman."

The whole of the Holy Father's reflection was based on this parallelism, because "the church has something of John the Baptist about her," even though, he immediately made clear, it's difficult to describe him. Jesus calls him "the greatest man ever born" but then "if we look at what he does" and "think about his life," noted Pope Francis, we realize that he is "a prophet who has passed, a man who has been great" before ending tragically.

Hence the invitation to ask who John the Baptist really was, allowing the protagonist to speak for himself. In fact, when "the scribes and Pharisees come to ask him to explain better who he is," he answers clearly: "I am not the Messiah. I am a voice, a voice crying in the wilderness." So the first thing we understand is that his interlocutors are "the wilderness," people with a "heart like that, with nothing," as the pope described them. He, on the other hand, is "a voice—a voice not word, because he is not the Word; the Word is someone else. He speaks but not of himself; he is the one who proclaims someone else who will come after him." In all this, the pope explained, we have "the mystery of John the Baptist" who "never takes over the word; the word is someone else. John is the one who points, the one who teaches" using the terms "after me … I am not who you think I am; someone is coming after me whose sandals I am not worthy to unlace." So "he is not the word"; he is instead "a voice indicating another." The whole meaning of his life "is to indicate another."

Continuing with his homily, Pope Francis stressed how the church chooses for the feast of St. John the Baptist "the longest days of the year, the days that have the most light, because in the darkness of that time John was the man of light; not his own light but a reflected light. Like a moon. And when Jesus began to preach," John's light began to fade, "to wane, diminish." He himself says so clearly when he speaks about his own mission: "He must increase and I must decrease."

So to sum up: "Voice, not word; light but not his own, John seems to be nothing." Here we have John the Baptist's "vocation," said the pope: "To annihilate himself. And when we consider this man who was so great, so powerful—they all believed he was the Messiah—when we consider how that life annihilated itself into the darkness of prison, we are looking at a mystery," a great mystery. In fact, he continued, "we don't know what it was like" for him in his final days. We are only told that he was killed and his head ended up "on a dish as a great gift from a dancer to an adulterer. I don't think we can get lower than that, in self-annihilation."

But we know what happened before that, during his time in prison. We know about "those doubts, the anguish he suffered." He reached the point of summoning his disciples and sending them "to ask the word: are you the one, or should we look for another?" For he was not spared "even darkness, pain about his life": does my life have any meaning, or have I made a mistake?

In short, said the pope, John the Baptist, could have boasted, could have felt important, but he didn't. He "only pointed; he felt himself to be a voice but not the word." That for Pope Francis is "the secret of John the Baptist." He "didn't want to be an ideologist." He was "a man who denied himself so that the word" might grow. And this is how his teaching applies today. The Holy Father wished: "We as church can ask today for the grace not to become an ideologically driven church," but to be "only the church *Dei Verbum religiose audiens et fidenter proclamans* [religiously hearing and faithfully proclaiming the Word of God]," he said, quoting the beginning of the [Second Vatican] Council's constitution on divine revelation. A "church that religiously listens to the word of Jesus and bravely proclaims it"; a "church without ideologies, without its own life"; a church that is mysterium lunae—the mystery of the moon—receiving her light from her bridegroom," which must dim her own light so that the light of Christ may shine.

Pope Francis did not doubt that "the model that John the Baptist offers us today" is of "a church always at the service of the word; a church that never takes anything for herself." And since the collect and the prayer of the faithful prayed for "the grace of joy" and "asked the Lord to make this church glad in her service to the word, to voice this word, to proclaim this word," the pope urged us to pray for "the grace to imitate John the Baptist: without our own ideas, without a gospel regarded as our own property"; to be "just a church that is a voice voicing the word, even to martyrdom."

THE CALL OF ABRAHAM

Tuesday, June 25, 2013
GEN 13:2, 5–18; MT 7:6, 12–14

The way to peace in the Middle East is the one indicated by the "wisdom" of Abraham, the common father in faith for Jews, Christians, and Muslims. That is what Pope Francis said in the Mass celebrated in the chapel of St. Martha's Guest House on Tuesday, June 25, referring to the "struggle for land" between Abraham and Lot described in chapter 13 of Genesis (2:5-18). "When I read this, I think about the Middle East and

I pray hard to the Lord to give us all wisdom: let's not fight—you here and I there—for peace," he said at the beginning of his homily. And, he added, Abraham reminds us that "none of us is a Christian by accident," because God calls us by name, with "a promise."

The pope reminded us that a promise lies at the heart of the story of Abraham, who is ready to leave his land "to go he didn't know where, but where the Lord told him to go." The Holy Father ran through his story, his journey to Egypt and his dispute and then peace with Lot over the land question. Pope Francis repeated the beautiful words of Genesis: "Then the Lord said to Abraham: 'Raise your eyes now, and look from the place where you are, northward and southward. Everything everywhere is yours; it will all belong to you and your descendants.'" And, he added, "this man, perhaps already in his nineties, looks at all that land and believes in the word of God who invited him to leave his own country. Believes. And then he goes and settles at the Oaks of Mamre, the place where the Lord will so often speak to him."

Abraham, the pope stressed, "left his country with a promise. And his journey is also a model for our journey. God calls Abraham, one person, and from this person he makes a people. If we turn to the book of Genesis, to the beginning, to the creation, we find that God creates the stars, he creates the plants, he creates the animals." All in the plural. But "he created man: in the singular. One. God always speaks to us in the singular, because he created us in his own image and likeness. And God speaks to us in the singular, as he did to Abraham, when he made him a promise and invited him to leave his country."

"We Christians," the pope continued, "have also been called one by one, in the singular. None of us is a Christian purely by accident, not one. It is a call to you, you, and you." It's a call "by name, with a promise: go ahead, I am with you; I am walking beside you."

"This," he explained, "was something Jesus also knew, when in his most difficult moments he turned to his Father," as he did "in the Garden of Olives. And at the end when he feels such great darkness," he says: "Father, why have you forsaken me?" So it's "always in relation to the Father who called him and sent him. Then when he left us on the day of the ascension, he says these beautiful words: I will always be with you, beside you: beside you, beside you, beside you. Always."

"God goes with us. God calls us by name. God promises us descendants," the pope reminded us. "And that's the Christian's security. It isn't an accident, it's a call. A call that makes us go forward. Being a Christian is a call to love, to friendship; a call to become a child of God, brother of Jesus, to become fruitful in the transmission of this call to others, to become an instrument of this call."

Of course, he recognized, "there are so many problems, so many difficult moments. Jesus himself went through so many, but always with that certainty: the Lord has called me, the Lord is with me, the Lord has made me a promise. But perhaps the Lord has made a mistake about me? The Lord is faithful, because he can never deny himself. He is faithfulness."

"Thinking of Abraham, in this passage of scripture, where he is anointed father for the first time, father of a people, let us also think of ourselves," the pope continued, "who have been anointed in baptism, and let us think about our Christian life." And to anyone who says, "Father, but I'm a sinner!" the pope replied that we are all sinners. The important thing is "to go forward, with the Lord. To go forward with that promise he has made to us, with that promise of fruitfulness; and to tell others, let others know that the Lord is with us, that the Lord has chosen us and he never leaves us on our own. That Christian certainty will do us good."

Pope Francis concluded with the hope that "the Lord may give us all the will to go ahead that Abraham had," even in the midst of difficulties. Go ahead with the certainty of Abraham, the certainty that "the Lord has called me; he has promised me so many wonderful things, and he is with me."

The Joy of Fatherhood

Wednesday, June 26, 2013
Gen 15:1–12, 17–18; Mt 7:15–20

The grace of fatherhood. This was the subject of Pope Francis' reflection during Mass this morning, Wednesday, June 26, in the chapel of St. Martha's Guest House. In particular, the pope stressed that "in order to become mature, all of us need to feel the joy of fatherhood." And he immediately added that this also goes for the celibate priesthood, because "fatherhood means giving life to others." So for priests it will be "pastoral fatherhood, spiritual fatherhood," which also means "giving life, becoming fathers."

In his homily, Pope Bergoglio referred to the readings for the day, focusing especially upon the first reading, from the book of Genesis (15:1-12, 17-18), which speaks of the covenant between Abraham and the Lord. Our father in faith, he explained, "felt that the Lord loved him, had promised him so much, but he also needed a son." He felt in himself "that cry of nature: I want to have a child." So, the pope recalled, he spoke to the Lord about his "desire to become a father," because "when a man doesn't feel this desire," there is something lacking in him, "something wrong."

And we see Abraham's fatherhood again, the pope recalled, at another moment. That "beautiful moment, in which he is preparing the sacrifice: he takes the animals, cuts them in two, but birds of prey come down. And I find this really moving," the pope confided, "to see this ninety-year-old with his stick in his hand defending the sacrifice, defending what is his own." That's an image which Pope Francis associates with "a father defending his family," "a father who knows" what it means "to defend his children." And this, he continued, "is a grace we priests must ask for: the grace of pastoral fatherhood, spiritual fatherhood." In fact, even though we all can have sins, even many sins, not having spiritual children, not becoming pastors means living a life that doesn't "reach its goal, but stops halfway."

The Holy Father then linked the subject of the homily to the presence of Cardinal Salvatore de Giorgi and his friends who were with him at the Mass. "Today," he said, "the Lord also gives us the grace of the biblical passage in this Mass, in which we are celebrating a father. I don't know what our dear friend Salvatore has done. But I'm sure he has been a father." And the presence of so many priests at his celebration is "a sign of that." By the way, he confided, before the beginning of the Mass, from his window in the Guest House, he had seen a group of priests arriving "with presents, so many things." And he had thought: "They are coming to greet their father." For, he explained, "these are actions whose meaning is clear." They are "the actions of children coming to their father." And for his part, Cardinal de Giorgi "can thank the Lord for this grace he has been given." A "good life," said the pope, referring to his ministry as bishop in various dioceses of Puglia and the archdiocese of Palermo, a life in which "the most beautiful thing is that he is a father; he bet on fatherhood and he won."

Then the Holy Father turned directly to the priests who were present. "Now," he said, using a football metaphor, "the ball is with you," because the Lord says that "every tree gives its own fruit, and if it is good the fruits will be good." And "you too," he urged them, "must carry on being fathers as priests, as you have seen this man do."

Finally, the pope summed up his reflection with three images. Two came directly from the first reading: "the image of Abraham asking for a son" and "the image of Abraham, stick in hand, defending his family." The third image is that of the old man Simeon in the temple who, he concluded, "when he receives the new life, breaks out into a spontaneous liturgy, a liturgy of joy."

Christians in Deed and in Truth

Thursday, June 27, 2013
Gen 16:1–12, 15–16; Mt 7:21–29

It's necessary to be "Christians in deed and in truth," whose lives are "founded on the rock that is Jesus," and not "Christians in word," who are superficial like the gnostics or rigid like the Pelagians. Resuming a subject dear to him, Pope Francis said this at the Mass celebrated this morning, Thursday, June 27, in the chapel of St. Martha's Guest House.

Inspired as usual by the day's readings, the pope's reflection began, in particular, with the passage from Matthew's gospel (7:21-29), where, the pope explained, "the Lord speaks to us about our foundation, the foundation of our Christian life." That means "we must build our house," or rather our life, on the rock that is Christ. When St. Paul speaks about the rock in the desert, he is referring to Christ, the pope stressed. Christ is the only rock "that can give us safety," so "we are invited to build our life upon this rock of Christ. There is no other."

In the gospel passage, recalled the Holy Father, Jesus also refers to those who believe they can build their lives on words alone: "Not everyone who says to me 'Lord, Lord' will enter the kingdom of heaven." But, said the pope, Jesus goes straight on to tell us to build "our house upon a rock." From this teaching, Pope Francis pointed out "two kinds of Christians in the history of the church." The first kind, of whom we need to beware, are "word-Christians," that is, those who merely repeat "Lord, Lord!" The second kind, the true ones, are "Christians in deed and in truth." He said there has always been "the temptation to live our Christianity away from the rock that is Christ; he is the only one who gives us the freedom to say 'Father' to God, the only one who supports us at difficult times." Jesus himself says so with particular examples: "The rain fell, the floods came, and the winds blew," but when "the foundation is a rock there is safety." On the other hand, when there are only "words, words fly away; they don't help." So in practice we end up with "the temptation to become these 'word-Christians,' in a Christianity without Jesus, a Christianity without Christ." And unfortunately "this has happened and happens today in the church."

This is a temptation that has arisen in all sorts of ways in the history of the church and given rise to various kinds of "Christians without Christ," among whom Pope Francis described just two. There is the "Christian-lite," who "instead of loving the rock, loves fine words, beautiful objects" and turns to a "god-spray," "a god for me," and who behaves "with superficiality and frivolity." There is still this temptation today, "superficial Christians who do believe in God" but not in Jesus Christ, "the one who gives you your foundation." The pope defined them as "modern gnostics," who yield to the temptation of a fluid Christianity.

Then the second kind are "those who believe Christian life" must "be taken so seriously" that they end up "confusing steadfastness and firmness with rigidity." The Holy Father defined "rigid Christians" as those "who think that to be Christians you have to be in mourning," always "taking everything very solemnly." These people attend carefully to the formalities, as the scribes and Pharisees did in Jesus' time. For the pope they are Christians for whom "everything is solemn. They are the Pelagians of today, who believe in the firmness of the faith." And they are convinced that "salvation comes from the way in which I do things": "I have to do it solemnly," without joy. The pope commented: "There are so many of them. They are not Christians, they are just wearing a Christian mask."

Altogether, two kinds of Christians—gnostics and Pelagians—"don't know Jesus, they don't know who the Lord is, they don't know what the rock is, they don't have the freedom of Christians." Consequently "they are without joy." The first lot "have a kind of superficial 'cheerfulness'"; the second lot "live life as a continual wake, and don't know what Christian joy is; they don't know how to enjoy the life Jesus gives us, because they don't know how to talk to him." So they don't find in Jesus "that strength which his presence gives." And as well as lacking joy, they "lack freedom."

The first lot, he continued "are slaves to superficiality" and the second lot are "slaves to rigidity"; they "aren't free," because "the Holy Spirit has no place in their lives." For "it is the Spirit who gives us freedom."

So this was the Lord's teaching today, according to Pope Francis: an invitation "to build our Christian life upon the rock that gives us freedom" and which "enables us to walk on with joy along his road, the way he proposes." Hence the pope's double exhortation, asking "the Lord for the grace not to become 'word-Christians,' either with 'gnostic superficiality' or 'Pelagian rigidity,'" so that we can "go ahead in life as Christians securely founded on the rock that is Jesus Christ and with the freedom the Holy Spirit gives us." This is a grace we should ask "especially from the Madonna. She," he concluded, "knows what it means to be founded upon a rock."

The Mystery of God's Patience

Friday, June 28, 2013
Gen 17:1, 9–10, 15–22; Mt 8:1–4

There are no "set terms for God's action in our lives," but we can be sure that, sooner or later, he will intervene "in his own way." So we must not give way to impatience or skepticism, also because when we get discouraged and "decide to come down from the cross, we always do so five minutes before the revelation." This invitation to know how to accept and recognize God's times was the pope's theme during the Mass celebrated this morning, Friday, June 28, in the chapel of St. Martha's Guest House.

God always walks with us "and that's certain," said the pope. "From the first moment of creation," he explained, "the Lord has been involved with us. He didn't create the world, man, woman and then just leave them. He created us in his own image and likeness." So since the beginning of time, there has been "that involvement by the Lord in our lives, in the lives of his people," because "the Lord is close to his people, very close. He himself says: what people on Earth has a god so close to them as I am to you?"

"The Lord's closeness," said Pope Francis, "is a sign of his love: he loves us so much that he wants to act together with us. Life is a road which he wants to walk with us. The Lord always comes into our life and helps us to walk on." But, he said, "when the Lord comes, it isn't always in the same way. There are no set terms for God's action in our lives. Sometimes he does it in one way and sometimes in another. But he always does act. There is always this encounter between us and the Lord."

In the passage from Matthew's gospel (8:1-4) in today's liturgy, "we have seen," said the Holy Father, "how the Lord suddenly comes into the life of that leper." The evangelist tells us: "When Jesus had come down from the mountain, great crowds followed him. And there was a leper who came to him and knelt before him, saying, 'Lord if you choose, you can make me clean.' He stretched out his hand and touched him, saying: 'I do choose. Be made clean!'" So Jesus intervenes "immediately: the prayer and then the miracle."

On the other hand, in the first reading, taken from the book of Genesis (17:1, 9-10, 15-22), "we see," the pope explained, "how the Lord comes into Abraham's life step by step, slowly. When Abraham was eighty-nine years old," God promised that he would have a son. "Today we have read that when he was ninety-nine years old, ten years later, he promised him a son. Ten years have passed. The wise men tell us: for the Lord one day is like a thousand years and a thousand years are like one day," stressed the pope.

"The Lord," he continued, "always goes his own way to come into our life. So often he comes so slowly that we risk losing patience: 'But when, Lord?' And we pray and pray, but he still doesn't come into our life." On the other hand, sometimes "we think about what the Lord has promised us, but it's such a great thing that we are a bit incredulous, a bit skeptical, and like Abraham we smile in secret." In fact the Genesis passage "tells us that Abraham hid his face and smiled. A touch of skepticism: 'But how can I, who am nearly a hundred years old, and my wife who is ninety have a child?'" And the pope added, "Sarah does so too at the Oaks of Mamre, when the three angels repeat the news to Abraham while she was hidden behind the door of the tent: surely she was spying to hear what the men were talking about, but that always happened... And when she heard that, she smiled. She smiled with skepticism."

The same thing also happens to us, as Pope Francis noted:

"How often, when the Lord doesn't come, doesn't work a miracle, and doesn't do what we want him to do, we become either impatient—'but he won't do it!'—or skeptical: 'he can't do it!'"

"The Lord takes his time," the pope continued, "but in this relationship with us, he too has so much patience. It's not just us who must have patience. God does and he waits for us. And he waits for us till the end of our lives, together with the good thief who recognized God at the very end of his life. The Lord walks with us, but so often he doesn't let himself be seen, as in the case of the disciples on the road to Emmaus."

"The Lord," the pope said again, "is involved in our lives, that's certain, but so often we don't see him. And that means we need patience. But the Lord who walks with us has so much patience with us: the mystery of God's patience, who walks in step with us along the road."

"Sometimes," Pope Francis explained, "things become so dark in our lives. There is so much darkness. And if we are in difficulties, we want to come down from the cross. And at that very moment—the night is darkest just before the dawn—always when we come down from the cross, we do so five minutes before the revelation. This is our moment of greatest impatience. Here Jesus' teaching can help us. On the cross he heard them challenging him: 'Come down, come down, come on!' So we need patience till the end, because he has patience with us. He always comes. He is involved with us. But he does so in his own way and when he thinks it best; he only says to us what he said to Abraham: 'Walk before me and be blameless, be irreproachable': that's exactly the right word."

The pope finished his homily by praying to the Lord to give us all the grace "to always walk in his presence trying to be irreproachable. That's the way with the Lord and he intervenes, but we must wait: wait for the moment, always walking on in his presence and trying to be irreproachable."

We Must Pray to the Lord with Courage

Monday, July 1, 2013
Gen 18:16–33; Mt 8:18–22

If we want to get something from God, we need to have the courage to "negotiate" with him through insistent prayer, a prayer of few words but with conviction. Thus Pope Francis spoke again about courage, which is needed in prayer to the Father with "all possible familiarity." And he gave as an example Abraham's prayer, his way of speaking with God as if he were negotiating with another man. That was what the pope invited reflection on by those taking part this morning, Monday, July 1, in the Mass celebrated in the chapel of St. Martha's Guest House.

The episode to which the pope referred is described in the book of Genesis (18:16-33), which relates Abraham's brave intercession to prevent the death of the righteous in the destruction of Sodom and Gomorrah. It was an example of familiarity and respect toward God. Abraham turns to God as he would to any man and poses the problem, insisting: "And if there were fifty righteous people? If there were forty, thirty, twenty, ten...?"

Abraham, recalled the pope, "was more than a hundred years old. He had been speaking with the Lord for almost twenty-five years and gained deep knowledge of him. And so the Lord turns and asks him, 'What shall I do with this sinful city?' Abraham feels the power of speaking face to face with the Lord, and tries to defend the city. He is insistent." He feels, the pope explained, that that land belongs to him and so he tries to save what is his own. But he also feels he must defend what belongs to the Lord.

"Abraham," said Pope Francis, "is brave and prays with

courage." Besides, what we find in the Bible is that "prayer must be brave." When we speak of courage "we always think of apostolic courage," which leads us "to go out and preach the gospel." But there is "also the courage to go before the Lord, to stand before the Lord, to go bravely to the Lord to ask for something." And "Abraham speaks to the Lord in a special way, with that courage."

The pope compared Abraham's prayer to "negotiating like a Phoenician," agreeing on a price and then trying to beat it down as low as possible. Abraham insists and "from fifty he manages to get the price down to ten," although he knew it wasn't possible to prevent the punishment of the sinful city. But he had to intercede to save "one righteous man, his cousin." With courage, with insistence, he kept on.

How often, recalled the pope, it will have happened to each of us to be praying for someone, saying: "Lord, I ask you for this, for this…" But "if we want the Lord to give us one grace," stressed the bishop of Rome, "we have to proceed with courage and do what Abraham did, with insistence. Jesus himself said we should pray like that." And to make the idea better understood, the pope referred to some episodes in the gospels showing how, by insisting, we can get what we ask from the Lord. That, he repeated, is "an attitude of prayer. St. Teresa speaks of prayer as negotiating with the Lord. And that's possible when there's familiarity with the Lord. And that's why she dared to pray that way. Insisting, with courage. True, it's tiring, but that's prayer. That's receiving a grace from God."

The pope then looked at how Abraham turns to the Lord: "He doesn't say, 'The poor things will be burned … forgive them.' But: 'Do you want to do this? Do you, who are so good, want to punish the just as well as the wicked? But no, you can't do that.' Abraham takes the arguments, the motivations from God's own heart. Moses does the same when the Lord wants to destroy the people: 'But no, Lord, don't do that because people will say: he brought them out of Egypt into the wilderness to kill them! You can't do that!' Convincing the Lord with the Lord's own virtues. Beautiful!"

So the suggestion is to go to the Lord's heart. "Jesus," said the pope, "teaches us: the Father knows things. Don't worry, the Father sends rain on the righteous and unrighteous, the just and the sinners. I'd like," he said, turning to those present, "all of us, from today, to take five minutes during the day to take up the Bible and slowly recite Psalm 102 [103], the psalm we recited between the two readings. 'Bless the Lord, O my soul, and all that is within me, bless his holy name. Bless the Lord, O my soul, and do not forget all his benefits, who forgives all your iniquity, who heals all your diseases, who saves your life from the pit, who crowns you with steadfast love and mercy.' Pray the whole psalm. And in this way we will learn what we ought to say to the Lord when we ask him for a grace."

Brave in Weakness

Tuesday, July 2, 2013
Gen 19:15–29; Mt 8:23–27

Temptation, curiosity, fear, and finally grace. These are four situations that occur when we find ourselves facing a difficulty. Pope Francis spoke about each of these during the Mass celebrated this morning, Tuesday, July 2, in the chapel of St. Martha's Guest House. He was reflecting on the texts from the day's liturgy (Genesis 19:15–29; Psalm 25; Matthew 8:23-28).

The Holy Father began his homily by referring to the special point in the day's liturgy, which, he said, makes us think of certain "conflictual" situations that are difficult to face. To reflect on these, he said, "will do us good."

The first attitude can be found in the slowness with which Lot responds to the angel's invitation telling him to hurry out of the city before it's destroyed. The pope was referring to the destruction of Sodom and Gomorrah, described in the book of Genesis, and the salvation Abraham gained for Lot and his family. The pope explained, "Lot had decided to leave the city. The evening before he had gone to his sons-in-law, who were to marry his daughters, to convince them to leave. So he had decided, but when the moment came to flee, he goes slowly, he doesn't hurry. Lot wanted to go away but slowly, slowly, slowly, even though the angel had told him to flee. That invitation is repeated so many times in the text: 'Flee, flee!'" According to the pope, Lot's attitude represents "the inability to detach oneself from evil, from sin. We don't want to leave; we have decided to go but something holds us back." Then the bishop of Rome pointed out Lot's final request to the Lord: "He succeeded in negotiating with the angel," in fact not to be forced to flee to the mountains but toward a smaller city that wasn't so far off. "I think," added the pope, to explain Lot's attitude, "perhaps there was the temptation to stay a bit closer" and that was what made him ask for this. In fact, "it's very difficult to cut ourselves off from a sinful situation." But "the voice of God says this to us: 'Flee. You can't fight there, because the fire and brimstone will kill you. Flee!' St. Teresa of the Child Jesus taught us that sometimes in the face of some temptations the only solution is to escape, not to be ashamed of escaping, recognize that we are weak and must flee. And in its simplicity our popular wisdom says as much, rather ironically: 'He who fights and runs away lives to fight another day' But it's escaping in order to go forward on the way of Jesus."

The second attitude also occurs in the story of Lot's flight.

"The angel," recalled the pope, "tells them not to look back: 'Flee and don't look back, go ahead.' This is also advice for us to overcome our nostalgia for sin." Recurrent advice in the word of God. For example, the Holy Father cited the flight of the people of God in the wilderness. They had everything; they were strong in the promises the Lord had made to them. They knew, however, that there would be difficulties in going ahead, but they were also aware of the Lord's constant presence beside them. Nevertheless they still continually felt nostalgia for "the onions of Egypt," forgetting, he recalled, that they had eaten those onions "at the table of slavery." But at that moment their nostalgia was so great that they forgot everything except the onions. "The angel's advice," said the pope, "is wise: don't look back. Go ahead!" And turning to those present, the pope said: In the prayer before Mass we asked the Lord for the grace not to fall back into the darkness of error: 'Lord, may we not fall back.' That will help us in this escape."

But sometimes it isn't enough to cut off all nostalgia "because," warned Pope Francis, "there is also the temptation to curiosity. And that's what happened to Lot's wife." So we must flee from sin without nostalgia and remember that "curiosity won't do, it does us harm." Flee and don't look back because "we are all weak and we must defend ourselves."

The third attitude about which Pope Francis spoke was that of fear. He referred to the episode in Matthew's gospel (8:23-27) of the apostles in the boat, when unexpectedly a storm blew up. "The boat was covered by the waves," the pope recalled. "'Save us, Lord, we are lost!' they cried. Fear, even that fear, is a temptation from the devil. To be afraid of going forward along the way of the Lord. We may reach the point of preferring to stand still, even though we are crushed by slavery, because we are afraid of going forward: 'I'm afraid of where the Lord will lead me.' Fear is not a good adviser. Jesus said it so many times: 'Don't be afraid!' Fear doesn't help us," said the pope.

The fourth attitude referred to was the grace of the Holy Spirit, which was manifested "when Jesus restored the lake to a great calm. And they were all full of amazement." So in the face of sin, in the face of nostalgia, of fear, it's necessary to "look to the Lord," stressed the pope, "contemplate the Lord," with that "beautiful amazement of a new encounter with the Lord. 'Lord, I have this temptation; I want to stay in this sinful situation. Lord I am curious to know how these things are. Lord, I'm afraid…,' but then the disciples looked to the Lord: 'Save us Lord, we are lost!' And then came the amazement of a new encounter with Jesus. Let us not be naïve or lukewarm Christians: let us be brave, courageous. Yes we are weak, but we must be brave in our weakness."

Touching His Wounds to Profess Jesus

Feast of St. Thomas the Apostle

Wednesday, July 3, 2013
Eph 2:19–22; Jn 20:24–29

We need to go out of ourselves and walk the streets to discover that the wounds of Jesus are still visible in the bodies of all our brothers and sisters who are hungry, thirsty, naked, humiliated, slaves, who are in prison or in hospital. And by touching these wounds, by stroking them, it's possible "to worship the living God in our midst."

The feast of St. Thomas the apostle gave Pope Francis the opportunity to return to an idea very close to his heart: putting our hands on Jesus' flesh. That's what Thomas did when he put his finger into the wounds of the risen Jesus. That was the main theme of his homily during the Mass celebrated this morning, Wednesday, July 3, in the chapel of St. Martha's Guest House.

After the readings (Ephesians 2:19-22; Psalm 116 [117]; John 20:24-29), the pope first of all spoke about the different attitude of the disciples "when after his resurrection, Jesus let himself be seen": some were happy and joyful, others doubted.

Thomas doubted. The Lord only showed himself to him eight days after that first appearance. "The Lord," said the pope, explaining this delay, "knows when and why he does things. He gives each of us the time he thinks right." He gave Thomas eight days. He wanted his wounds to still be visible on his body, despite the fact that it was "shining, very beautiful, full of light," because, recalled the pope, the apostle had said that unless he put his finger into the Lord's wounds, he wouldn't believe. "He was stubborn! But the Lord," commented the pope, "wanted a stubborn person to make us understand something even greater. Thomas saw the Lord and was invited to put his finger into the wound of the nails, and to put his hand into Jesus' side. But then he didn't say: 'It's true, the Lord has risen.' No, he went further and said: 'My Lord and my God.' He is the first of the disciples to confess Christ's divinity after the resurrection. And he worshiped him."

From this confession, explained the bishop of Rome, we can understand what God's intention was: using Thomas's disbelief to bring him to affirm not just Jesus' resurrection but his divinity. "And Thomas," said the pope, "worships the Son of God. But in order to worship, in order to find God, the Son of God, he had to put his finger into the wounds and his hand into Jesus' side. That's the way." There is no other.

Naturally "in the history of the church," the pope continued, "there have been some mistakes about the way to God. Some people thought that the living God, the God of the Christians," could be found by going "higher in meditation." But that's "dangerous; how many get lost on that way and never get there?" said the pope. "Yes, perhaps they reach the knowledge of God but not of Jesus Christ, the Son of God, the second person of the Trinity," he continued. They don't get there. This is the way of the gnostics: they are good, they work at it, but that isn't the right way; it's very complicated, and it doesn't lead to a good end.

Others, continued the Holy Father, "have thought that to reach God we have to be good, mortify ourselves, live austerely, and have chosen the way of penance, penance and fasting. These didn't reach the living God either, they didn't get to Jesus Christ the living God." These, he added, "are the Pelagians, who think they can get there through their own efforts. But Jesus tells us this: 'We've seen Thomas on the way.' But how can I find Jesus' wounds today? I can't see them as Thomas did. You can find Jesus' wounds by doing works of mercy, giving help to the body, to the body and also the soul—but I stress the body—of your wounded brother, because he is hungry, because he is thirsty, because he is naked, because he is humiliated, because he is enslaved, because he is in prison, because he is in hospital. Those are the wounds of Jesus today. And Jesus asks us to make an act of faith in him by means of these wounds."

It isn't enough, added the pope, to set up "a foundation to help everyone" or "to do a lot of good works to help them." All that is important, but it would be mere philanthropy. Rather, said Pope Francis, "we must touch the wounds of Jesus, we must stroke the wounds of Jesus. We must cure the wounds of Jesus with tenderness. We must literally kiss the wounds of Jesus." The life of St. Francis, he recalled, changed when he kissed the leper, because "he touched the living God and worshiped him." "What Jesus asks us to do with our works of mercy," concluded the pope, "is what Thomas asked to do: to enter into the wounds."

The Freedom of the Children of God

Thursday, July 4, 2013
Gen 22:1–19; Mt 9:1–8

If there were an "identity card" for Christians, freedom would certainly figure among the characteristic traits. In his homily at the Mass celebrated this morning, Thursday, July 4, in the chapel of St. Martha's Guest House Pope Francis explained that the freedom of the children of God is the fruit of reconciliation with the Father brought about by Jesus. He took upon himself the sins of us all and redeemed the world by his death on the cross. No one, declared the pope, can take that identity away from us.

The Holy Father's reflection was based on the passage from Matthew's gospel (9:1-8), which relates the miracle of the healing of the paralyzed man. The pope dwelled on the feelings that must have shaken the sick man's soul when he was brought to Jesus on his bed and heard him say: "Take heart, son; your sins are forgiven."

Those who were with Jesus at that moment and heard his words "said, 'This man is blaspheming; only God can forgive sins.' And to make them understand, Jesus asked them, 'Which is easier: to forgive or to heal?' And he healed the man. Jesus, says St. Peter, went about doing good, healing everyone, curing everyone."

But, continued the bishop of Rome, "when Jesus healed a sick person he wasn't just a healer. When he taught people—think of the Beatitudes—he wasn't just a teacher, a moral preacher. When he lambasted the hypocrisy of the Pharisees and Sadducees, he wasn't a revolutionary who wanted to drive out the Romans, No, these things that Jesus did—healing, teaching, his strong words against hypocrisy—were just signs, signs of something more that Jesus was doing: forgiving sins."

Reconciling the world in Christ in the Father's name: "that is Jesus' mission. Everything else—the cures, the teaching, the rebukes—are only signs of that greater miracle which is the re-creation of the world. A beautiful prayer of the church says: 'O Lord, you who wonderfully created the world have redeemed it even more wonderfully, re-created it.'" So reconciliation is the re-creation of the world, and Jesus' ultimate mission, added the pope, is the redemption of all us sinners: "Jesus does this not by words, not by gestures, not by walking along the road, no! He does it in his own flesh. He, God, becomes one of us, man, to heal us from within." But, asked the pope, "can we say that Jesus became a sinner? It's not quite like that, because he couldn't sin. Paul puts it right: he didn't become a sinner, he became sin (2 Corinthians 5:21). He took all sin upon himself. And that is beautiful; that is the new creation"; it's "Jesus who comes down from glory and lowers himself to the point of death, death on a cross. That is his glory and that is our salvation. And the cross in the end becomes sin (2 Corinthians 5:21)."

Referring to the first reading at the Mass, taken from the book of Genesis (22:1-19), the pope recalled that whereas Abraham replied immediately to his son Isaac who had asked him about the victim for the sacrifice, the Father didn't reply "to Jesus who said 'My Father.' And he said: 'Father, why have you forsaken me?'" Jesus "had become sin in order to set us free (cf. 2 Corinthians 5:21)." That's "the greatest miracle," through which Jesus made us children of God and gave us the freedom of children. And that's why "we can say 'Father.' Otherwise we couldn't have said it."

"That," added the pope, "is Jesus' great miracle. He set us free who were slaves to sin"; he healed us. "It does us good to think about this," he continued, "and to think how lovely it is to be children. This freedom of being children is beautiful because the Son is at home. Jesus has opened the door of the house to us; now we are at home. Now we can understand that word of Jesus: 'Take heart, son; your sins are forgiven.'" That's the root of our courage: I am free, I am a child; my Father loves me and I love the Father. Let us ask the Lord for the grace to understand well this work of his."

God "reconciled the world to himself in Christ," he concluded, "entrusting us with the word of reconciliation. And the grace to carry this word of reconciliation forward strongly, with the freedom of children. We are saved in Jesus Christ" and no one can ever take that grace away from us.

MERCY, FEAST, AND MEMORY

Friday, July 5, 2013
GEN 23:1–4, 19; 24:1–8, 62–67; MT 9:9–13

Let Jesus' mercy look at us; feast with him; keep alive the "memory" of the moment when we found salvation in our lives. This was the triple invitation that issued from Pope Francis' reflection during the Mass celebrated this morning, Friday, July 5, in the chapel of St. Martha's Guest House.

In his homily the pope commented on the passage from Matthew's gospel (9:9-13), in which the author speaks of his own conversion: that of a tax collector whom Jesus calls to become one of the Twelve. The message Jesus wants to give, the pope explained, was taken "from the tradition of the people of Israel. A prophetic message, but one that the people have always found difficult to understand: I desire mercy and not sacrifice." In fact, our God is a God of mercy. We can see it clearly in the story of Matthew, explained Pope Francis, which "isn't a parable": it's a historical fact; "it happened."

Pope Francis recalled the image of Jesus walking among "those who received the money for the taxes, which they then passed on to the Romans." These people, he said, were regarded as despicable, because they were "doubly sinners: attached to money and also traitors to their country." Among them was Matthew, "the man sitting on the tax bench." Jesus looks at him, and that look makes him feel "something new inside, something he had never experienced." "Jesus' look," explained the Holy Father, arouses an inner "amazement, makes him feel Jesus' invitation: Follow me." And at that very moment Matthew is "full of joy." In short, commented the pope, recalling Caravaggio's famous painting [The Calling of St. Matthew], Matthew needs "only a moment" to understand that look had changed his life forever. At that very moment, "Matthew says yes; he leaves everything and goes off with the Lord. It's the moment of mercy received and accepted: I am coming with you."

The first moment of meeting, which is "a deep spiritual experience," is followed by another: a party. The gospel story continues with the description of Jesus sitting at table with tax collectors and sinners, for "a feast," continued Pope Francis, "with all those who weren't exactly the cream of society"; on the contrary, "they were outcasts from society." But for the pope this "is the contradiction of God's feast: the Lord feasts with sinners," whereas he seldom does so with the righteous. The pope then recalled chapter 15 of Luke's gospel, where it is clearly said that there will be more joy in heaven over one sinner who repents than over ninety-nine righteous who need no repentance. And further on in the same chapter, we have the story of the father who makes a feast for the return of his prodigal son. So for Pope Francis, feasting is "very important," because it is celebrating an encounter with Jesus, God's mercy: "He looks at someone with mercy, changes their life and has a party."

But life is not all feasting. Pope Bergoglio knows that very well. As he confided during the Mass, in his long experience as a priest and bishop he had often been asked: "Father, after these two moments, the amazement of meeting and the party, will the rest of life go on being just one party?" The answer, said the pope, is no, because "the party is to begin on a new road," but then there has to be "daily work, which needs to be nourished by the memory of that first meeting." This was just what happened in Matthew's life, "who did this work, going out to preach the gospel." In this case, said the pope, it isn't about "a moment" but "a time" that goes on "until the end of life."

But, asked the pope, what do we need to remember? "That meeting with Jesus which changed my life, when he had mercy, was so kind to me," was his reply. "And he also told me: invite your friends who are sinners, because we'll have party." In fact, the memory of that mercy and that feast "gives strength to Matthew and to all" who have decided to follow Christ and "go forward." That, added the pope, needs to be always remembered, as when we blow on the coals to keep the fire alive.

Continuing with his theme, the Holy Father pointed out "two moments and a time: the moment of meeting, when Jesus looks at Matthew with that look of mercy, and the moment of feasting, to set out on the road; and the time of memory, memory of those two events." All Jesus' preaching was going about "through the streets to seek out the poor, the sick" to "have a party with them." A party to which he also invited sinners, drawing a lot of criticism upon himself. But we know his answer: "Go and learn what this means: 'I desire mercy, not sacrifice.' For I have come to call sinners, not the righteous." That is to say, concluded Pope Francis, "those who think they are righteous, who stew in their own juice. He came for us sinners."

Renewal without Fear

Saturday, July 6, 2013
Gen 27:1–5, 15–29; Mt 9:14–17

Pope Francis gave an invitation to let ourselves be renewed by the Holy Spirit, not to be afraid of what is new, not to fear renewal in the church's life, during the Mass this morning, Saturday, July 6, in St. Martha's Guest House, the last one before the summer break.

Commenting on the gospel for the day (Matthew 9:14-16), the pope focused on the innovative spirit that drove Jesus. "For example," he noted, "Jesus says, 'The law allows us to hate our enemies, hate your enemies; but I tell you pray for your enemies, don't hate.'" He also applied this precept to things that didn't seem right to him. For example, as the gospel passage relates to the question of fasting. "Jesus," explained the pope, "advised fasting, but with a certain freedom. In fact some of John's disciples asked him: why do we fast and your disciples don't?" The fact is that "the doctrine of the law is enriched, renewed by Jesus. Jesus makes all things new, he renews things." For he is "the same Jesus who says: 'I make all things new.' As if it were his vocation to renew everything. And that is the Reign of God which Jesus preaches. It's a renewal, a true renewal. And this renewal is first of all in our hearts."

Pope Francis reminded those who think Christian life consists only in fulfilling a series of requirements that "being a Christian means letting ourselves be renewed by Jesus in a new life." To be a good Christian, he said, "it isn't enough to say: 'I go to Mass every Sunday from 11 till noon, and I do this and this,' as if it were a collection of duties. Christian life is not a mish-mash of things. It's a harmonious whole, work of the Holy Spirit. He renews everything. He renews our hearts, our lives and makes us live differently," as a whole. "We can't be piecemeal, part-time Christians," said the pope. "Being part-time Christians doesn't work; we have to be full-time Christians."

Being a Christian "doesn't mean doing things," repeated the bishop of Rome. "It means letting ourselves be renewed by the Holy Spirit. Or to use Jesus' words, it means becoming new wine. The novelty of the gospel is a novelty in the law belonging to salvation history." It's a newness that goes beyond ourselves "and renews structures. That's why Jesus says: 'For new wine you need new wineskins.' In Christian life and also in the life of the church, there are worn-out structures. And it's necessary to renew them. The church has always been attentive to dialogue with different cultures" and tries to renew itself, to respond to the different requirements of places, times, and people. This is work "that the church has always done, from the very beginning. Let us recall the first theological dispute: in order to become a Christian is it necessary to carry out all the Jewish practices or not? No, they said no."

Gentiles can also enter the church and receive baptism, the pope explained. The church, he added, has always proceeded like that, letting the Holy Spirit renew structures. And it has taught us "not to be afraid of the newness of the gospel, not to be afraid of the newness the Holy Spirit creates in us, not to be afraid of the renewal of structures. The church is free. The Holy Spirit carries it forward. That's what Jesus teaches us in the gospel today: the freedom necessary always to find the gospel's newness in our lives and also in structures. The freedom to choose new wineskins for this renewal. A Christian is a free man or woman, with the freedom of Jesus Christ. He or she isn't a slave of habit, of structures." The one who carries out this renewal, the pope continued, has always been the Holy Spirit. So the pope recalled the day of Pentecost, emphasizing the presence of Mary with the apostles: "Where the mother is the children are safe." Concluding his homily, the bishop of Rome invited us to ask for "the grace not to be afraid of the newness of the gospel, not to be afraid of the renewal brought by the Holy Spirit, not to be afraid to get rid of worn-out structures that imprison us. And if we are afraid, we know that our mother is with us." Like children who take refuge in their mother's arms, "when we are afraid we can go to her. And as the ancient antiphon says, she 'covers us with her cloak, with her motherly protection.'"

Pope Francis

❧

MORNING HOMILIES

<small>APOSTOLIC JOURNEY TO RIO DE JANEIRO ON THE
OCCASION OF THE XXVIII WORLD YOUTH DAY</small>

LIKE CLAY POTS
Sumaré Residence

Thursday, July 25, 2013

We must never forget that we are like "clay pots" in which to keep the treasure God has given us by the revelation of the mystery of the incarnation. When we forget, we delude ourselves that we are something other than clay. Then everything rebels and we think we are greater than we are. In his homily at the Mass celebrated on Thursday morning, July 25, in the residence of the papal suite, with a tightly packed group of bishops, priests, and seminarians of the diocese, Pope Francis said this was a danger especially for religious, priests, bishops: all those, he said, who receive this gift to keep, without forgetting the enormous difference between the greatness of the gift received and the littleness of the one receiving it. If we lose sight of this relationship, we lose our balance and end up denying our mission to serve the people of God, which has appointed us guardians of the mystery. Then careerism worms its way in, "which has done so much harm to the church." To regain our balance, he concluded, it's necessary above all to rediscover the sacrament of confession.

THE TREASURE AND THE CLAY

Thursday, July 25, 2013
2 COR 4:7–15; MT 20:20–28

Before starting his day's activities in Rio, Pope Francis celebrated Mass in the chapel of his suite in the Residence, attended by a densely packed group of Brazilian bishops, priests, and seminarians. Human frailty, or rather the awareness of human frailty in the face of the immensity of God's mystery, was the theme of his homily, delivered in Spanish. We are like clay pots guarding an immense treasure: beware of forgetting that, because you might end up deluding yourself that you are something you are not and yielding to those flatteries that do so much harm to the church.

This is a risk affecting everyone, even bishops. And the pope described it, taking his cue from the first letter of St. Paul to the Corinthians, "who had no words to explain the mystery of the incarnation. He had to go ahead and dismantle the ideological systems that didn't explain this great mystery well. He had to fight against gnostic tendencies that came from the Essenes or against the nominalist Pelagianism of the orthodox-Pharisee tendency." He didn't know but "he always moved between two things: the greatness of Jesus Christ, whom he called 'my Lord,' and our littleness, the littleness of those who had been chosen to proclaim the gospel."

So at the heart of the matter there is the tension between the value of the treasure that has been given and the fragility of the container, "a simple clay pot." This applies "to all of us, the consecrated, religious, priests, and bishops," said the pope, because "we have received a gift" and we are all "clay pots." The problem is not to lose the balance in this tension. It may happen that men and women, even in the church, "receive the gift, know they are made of clay, but in the course of their lives they become so enthusiastic that they forget they are made of clay or they forget the gift is such a great one. Then that tension loses the balance that does us so much good." And the temptation creeps in "to decorate the clay pot, to paint it, beautify it. So we begin to deceive ourselves and believe we are no longer made of clay."

Up to a point, even the apostles fell into that worldly delusion, so that they began discussing who was the most important. But "Jesus stopped them: 'It shall not be so among you: the servant is one who serves.'" The church "has suffered greatly," said Pope Francis, "and continues to suffer greatly every time one of those called to receive the treasure in a clay pot hoards the treasure, devotes himself to changing the nature of the clay, trying to make it better, no longer clay." We are made of clay "right to the end; no one can escape from that. Jesus saves us in his own way, but not by the human way of a conjuring trick, by appearances, by having an important job. That's where careerism creeps into the church and does so much harm."

But how can we become aware of this approaching danger? In order to understand it, said the Holy Father, we need to think about how we make our confession, if we really face the truth "told by ourselves." And how can we recognize the greatness of the gift? By asking ourselves, explained the pope, if we are capable of worshiping Jesus and if we do worship him. So, he concluded, "how we make our confession will tell us whether we are aware that we are made of clay; and how we pray, if we worship in prayer, will tell us that we realize this is a gift, a great gift."

The Wisdom of Grandparents
Saints Joachim and Ann, parents of Mary

Friday, July 26, 2013
Sir 44:1, 10–15; Mt 13:16–17

The world needs wisdom. The wisdom those can offer who are a link in the chain of world history. A history that has already begun but whose future still remains to be written. In the homily of the Mass celebrated on Friday morning, July 26, in the Sumaré Residence with some fellow Jesuits living in Brazil, Pope Francis resumed a subject that often came up during these days in Rio. The subject was the need to rediscover the richness of collaboration between the generations. So taking the occasion of the feast of the parents of the Virgin Mary, Joachim and Anna, the pope again praised the role of grandparents, their being a fount of wisdom to hand on to their grandchildren so that they can build the future with deeper awareness.

"Today in Brazil," said the pope, "we are celebrating the feast of grandparents. Grandparents have this: when they see their grandchildren they bet on life and on the future; they want the best for their grandchildren. Today it will do us good to think about our grandparents," about how much they loved us and the wisdom they passed on to us. "Grandparents," he added, "are those in a country who must pass on wisdom, aren't they? And leave it as a legacy." So the pope invited us to ask the Lord to bless grandparents, since "they are a link in the life chain." And he asked the Lord "to give us the grace to grow old with wisdom; to grow old with dignity, so that we can either be 'material' grandparents or the ordained could be spiritual grandparents" able to pass on wisdom. And to strengthen the idea, the pope used the example of good wine, "which improves when it is older: it gets better! Bad wine becomes vinegar. We can be like good wine. We can grow old wisely so that we can pass on wisdom."

But that's not enough, because we must "also ask for the grace to believe that the story doesn't end with us, and it didn't even begin with us: the story goes on," stressed the bishop of Rome. And then he prayed that the Lord "may also give us a little humility, to be able to be a link in the chain" for the transmission of the faith.